Nelson History

Public Health and Medicine

Books are to be returned on or before
the last date bel...

John D Clare

Nelson

Thomas Nelson and Sons Ltd
Nelson House Mayfield Road
Walton-on-Thames Surrey
KT12 5PL UK

51 York Place
Edinburgh
EH1 3JD UK

Nelson Blackie
Wester Cleddens Road
Bishopbriggs
Glasgow
G64 2NZ UK

Thomas Nelson (Hong Kong) Ltd
Toppan Building 10/F
22A Westlands Road
Quarry Bay Hong Kong

Thomas Nelson Australia
102 Dodds Street
South Melbourne
Victoria 3205 Australia

Nelson Canada
1120 Birchmount Road
Scarborough Ontario
M1K 5G4 Canada

© John D. Clare 1994

First published by Thomas Nelson and Sons Ltd 1994

ISBN 0-17-435099-6
NPN 9 8 7 6 5 4 3 2 1

Printed in Spain.

Acknowledgements
The publishers are grateful to the following for permission to reproduce copyright material:

Arts Libraries and Museums Department, Darlington: p.35 (bottom); BBC: p.51; Biblioteca Medicea Laurenhania: p. 20; Bodleian: p.18 (bottom right); Bridgeman: p.22, 23, 26, 27 (top); British Library: p.18 (top left), 18 (top right); British Museum : p.5 (upper), 5 (lower) 9, 11; CADW: p.12 (middle right); Daily Mirror: p.56 (2); Derek Penman: p.55; Frank Graham/Ron Embleton: p.12 (top left), 12 (bottom right); Hulton Deutsch Collection: p.17, 24, 25 (bottom left), 29, 34 (top), 34 (bottom), 35 (top), 33, 36, 39, 42, 43 (top left), 44, 48, 49, 53 (top), 54 (top left); Institute of Archaeology, Oxford: p.6 (upper), 6 (lower); John Urling Clark: p.4, 47; Mansell Collection: p.22, 27 (bottom); Mary Evans: p.30, 46; Norman Meredith: p.21; Norwich Castle Museum: p.14; Public Record Office: p.52; Punch: p.53 (bottom), 57 (top), 57 (bottom); Ronald Grant: p.58 (4); Royal College of Surgeons: p.25 (top); S Gibson / M H Brown: p.13; Tate Gallery: p.43 (bottom); Trustees of the Wellcome Trust: p.19; Wellcome Trust: p.25 (bottom right); York Archaeology Trust: p.12 (middle left).

Although every effort has been made to trace original sources and copyright holders, this has not been possible in all cases. The publishers will be pleased to rectify any such omission in future editions.

Contents

Iron Age houses
At Chiltern Open Air Museum in Buckinghamshire, archaeologists have built a reconstruction of an Iron Age house. Are projects like this of any use to a historian studying public health in Iron Age Britain?

Knowledge and understanding

These questions will help you to develop some first thoughts about the basic question: what is public health?

1 List all those things that make or keep you healthy. Stop at 40 items. Analyse them, putting them into different categories (groups of similar items). Some of the items will be personal health care (such as brushing your teeth); others will be public (e.g. hospitals). Studying the list a different way, you will be able to identify environmental factors (street cleaners) and medical factors (doctors), curative measures (medicines) and preventative measures (sewers), and private and state-funded services. Some items on your list may fall into more than one category.

2 Write down a list of the criteria (principles) by which you would identify whether a country has a public health system. You will be asked to change and improve this definition as your knowledge grows. Must a public health system be provided by the government?

3 Public health (the health of the public) is often treated as an aspect of the history of medicine. Do you agree?

The Iron Age in Britain began with the coming of the first Celtic settlers from France in the sixth century B.C. The Celts brought iron smelting and enamelling, two-wheeled war-chariots and a 'heroic way of life … rich in heroic tales, songs and legends'. Their Druid priests made human sacrifices; Hallowe'en is a left-over of the terrifying Celtic New Year's Eve festival.

However, little evidence about health in Iron Age Britain has survived. Information has to be collected from what one historian has described as 'little-known, diverse and scattered' remains. One of the skills of the historian is to evaluate that information.

The Bog Man

In 1984 the body of a man was found preserved in the peat of Lindow Moss in Cheshire. His skull had been smashed in, his throat had been slit and he had been strangled. The body was radio-carbon dated at about 300 B.C. The information in **Sources 2–3** is from *The Bog Man* (1987), by Don Brothwell, the biological adviser during the investigation which followed.

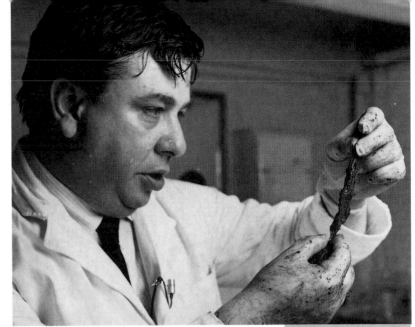

SOURCE 3

Studying the gut
His last meal had been cooked bran gruel (a thin porridge) made from emmer (a kind of wheat), barley, wild oats and grass seeds. In the gruel were grains of sand, the spores of fungi which had infected the plants, and the hairs of small animals (e.g. mice) which had lived in the grain store. Investigators found the eggs of two intestinal worms – whipworm and maw worm – in large numbers.

SOURCE 2

Lindow Man
There was no evidence of fleas or lice. His hair had been trimmed with a pair of scissors, and his nails were polished and manicured. He might have suffered from rheumatism; his lower backbone showed slight strains from pulling and lifting. Otherwise, he seemed to be healthy.

Danebury Iron Age hill-fort

Danebury, in Hampshire, was a hill-fort settlement of perhaps 300 people. The facts in this Datapoint are taken from B. Cunliffe, *Danebury* (1983). They were discovered during the archaeological investigation of the fort.

SOURCE 4

Excavating building number CS20

Most houses at Danebury were round, one-door buildings, between 6 and 9 metres in diameter. They were skilfully built, with wattle-and-daub walls, thatched roofs and floors of rammed chalk. The archaelogists found no evidence that they left their rubbish, or kept animals, in their houses.

Cunliffe writes, 'It would be unwise to regard them all as houses in the sense that each was inhabited by a single family. This might be the case, [but they were probably] different functional units, for sleeping, cooking, weaving, storage etc., providing for the needs of extended family groups … [One house] may have provided centralised cooking facilities for those houses without their own hearth …'.

SOURCE 5

Settlement plan
This plan shows the position of all the post-holes and wall-slots. It is possible to make out where the roads ran, and some of the circular house bases.

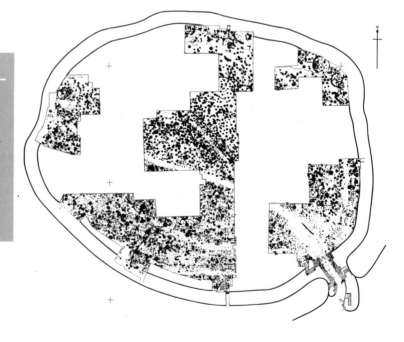

Average age at death

	Men	Women
Danebury	29.5	26.5
Roman Empire	35	28
Britain in 1991	73.2	78.1

Stature of Danebury inhabitants

Men	1.64 m	(range 1.57–1.75 m)
Women	1.56 m	(range 1.50–1.60 m)

Roman descriptions

Much of what we know about the Iron Age in Britain comes from Roman writers (**Sources 6–7**). Their evidence is both biased and from the later Celtic period. According to one Roman writer, the peoples of Britain were barbarians who lived beyond the civilised world and were 'absolutely unknown' until the Emperor Claudius conquered them in A.D. 43.

SOURCE 6

The Britons – I

All the Britons wear their hair long; they keep the rest of their body clean-shaven apart from their top lips. Wives are shared between groups of ten or twelve men.

Caesar, *Gallic War*, c. 54 B.C.
A military description of Caesar's invasion of Britain in 55–54 B.C.

SOURCE 7

The Britons – II

They are taller than the Gauls, and not so yellow-haired … They are well supplied with milk, but do not know how to make cheese; they know nothing of planting crops … Their cities are the forests, for they cut down trees and fence in large circular enclosures in which they build huts and pen their cattle, but not for long. The weather tends to rain rather than snow. Mist is very common …

Strabo, *Geography*, c. 7 B.C.
Strabo was a Roman writer. It is now known that, on the contrary, Britain was the 'granary of Europe'. Some historians think that the Romans invaded to secure this supply of corn.

Knowledge and understanding

These questions will help you to investigate and evaluate the evidence about health in Iron Age Britain.

1 Divide into small groups of two or three. Take either Lindow Man (Sources 2–3) or the Danebury settlement (**Datapoint: Danebury Iron Age hill-fort** on page 6) or the Roman descriptions of Iron Age Britons (Sources 6–7). Discuss in your groups the following:
a What do your sources tell you about people's health in Iron Age Britain? (Suggest a number of ideas.)
b For each idea, decide whether this idea is certainly true, possibly true, or a remote possibility.

2 As a whole class, share and debate your findings. On what issues do the sources agree? In which areas do they contradict each other?

3 Which of the sources proved to be the most valuable for the study of health in Iron Age Britain?

Graeco-Roman ideas about health

It is important to understand that Celtic Britain was unknown and irrelevant to the civilised world (when Caesar reported that he had invaded 'the Ultimate Isles', some Romans refused to believe they existed). The concept of public health was developed in Ancient Greece, while the Britons were still running around in animal skins and painting themselves blue. Greek ideas influenced public health and medicine for the next two thousand years.

The Greeks were the first people to seek natural causes for disease. Hippocrates of Cos (c. 460–377 B.C.), to whom are attributed 70 books on medicine, is still known as the Father of Medicine. By 300 B.C., Erasistratos, the Father of Physiology (the study of how the body works), was stressing the importance of hygiene, diet and exercise for a healthy life. The Greeks were the first people to study the connection between environment and health (**Source 8**).

Greek philosophers believed that the earth was made of four elements linked by heat and moisture. Greek doctors

SOURCE 8

Factors affecting health

Whoever wishes to follow the science of medicine must proceed as follows. On arriving in a town he does not know, he must examine its position with respect to the winds and the sunrise. He must carefully think about the inhabitants' drinking water … and the soil. The people's way of life is also important, whether they are heavy drinkers and eaters and do little, or athletic, eating much and drinking little … He must know the changes of the seasons and the risings and settings of the stars … In this way he will gain the greatest success.

Hippocrates, *Airs, Waters and Places*.
(Most of the books in the Hippocratic collection were probably not written by Hippocrates, but by his disciples, during the course of the fourth century B.C.)

SOURCE 9

The four humours

Perfect health occurs when the person stands in the centre of the diagram – i.e. when the four humours are perfectly balanced. If changes in heat or moisture cause a change in the person's position, then an imbalance of the humours occurs and the person falls ill.

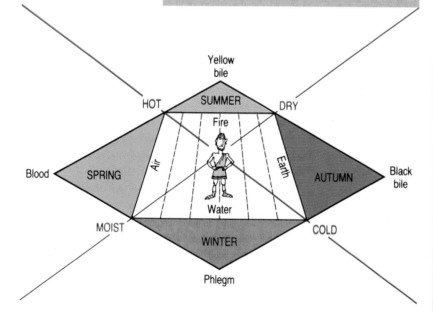

developed this idea into the theory that the human body contained four liquids, which they called humours (**Source 9**).

Greece was conquered by the Romans in the second century B.C., but this did not mean the end of Greek civilisation and ideas. Greek doctors were taken back to Italy as the slave doctors of Roman noble families. In this way Greek theories about medicine came to be adopted throughout the Roman Empire. The most influential doctor of Roman times – Galen (*c.* A.D. 130–200) – was a Greek.

Greek and Roman doctors believed that health was achieved when a person's heat, moisture and humours were all perfectly balanced. To bring a sick person back to health, they might bleed or purge the patient to reduce the amount of blood or black bile. Sometimes they used special diets to try to affect the patient's humours, heat and moisture – beans were a laxative and restricted the blood; hot, thick barley soup cured chest diseases. Baths, exercise and sleep were likewise recommended to cool, heat, wet or dry the patient (**Source 10**).

SOURCE 10

To keep the body balanced

In winter, it is best to counteract the cold … by eating dry, warming foods [such as] wheat bread … and roast meat … Drink only a little, undiluted wine. Exercise as often as possible in every way you can; running on the double track … wrestling … brisk walks after exercise and short walks in the sun after dinner … A hot bath is good for you. Have sexual intercourse more often …

In summer … eat smaller amounts of softer, purer food; drink smooth, white, diluted wines … Avoid over-eating and drink a lot … Reduce sexual intercourse to a minimum, take lukewarm baths … and take only short strolls after dinner.

Hippocrates, *A Programme for Health*.

The first system of public health

It is usually the Romans who are credited with having developed the first public health system. In Rome, this included:

- aqueducts which brought into the city 80 gallons (364 litres) of water per person per day (twice the ration Londoners receive today);
- *thermae* (baths) with not only swimming baths, but also gymnasia, gardens, reading rooms and extra-hot baths for invalids;
- *valetudinaria* (hospitals) for wounded soldiers and the sick, weak and aged poor.

- a welfare system with a monthly handout of free grain to every citizen and support for poor children and orphans;
- 14 *archiatri* (public doctors) who treated the poor free of charge;
- public latrines, a sewage system and a team of slaves who every night cleaned the streets and latrines;

What makes a society put money and effort into public health? The sources on page 10 suggest a number of different reasons why the Romans developed a state system of health. These ideas will provide a useful yardstick for comparison when we study the reasons for the introduction of state public health in nineteenth-century Britain.

SOURCE 12

Keeping the army healthy

The army can be kept healthy by the siting of camps, purity of water, temperature, medicine and exercise ... If a number of soldiers are allowed to stay in one place too long in the summer or autumn, then they suffer from the effects of polluted water, and are made miserable by the smell of their own excrement. The air is made unhealthy ... and they catch serious diseases.

Vegetius, *A Brief Account of War*, c. A.D. 385.
Vegetius was a Roman general.

SOURCE 13

The aqueducts

The result of this care [for the aqueducts] is seen in the improved health of the city ... The appearance of the city is clean and altered; the air is purer; and the causes of the unhealthy atmosphere, which gave the air of the city such a bad reputation in the past, are now removed.

Frontinus, *About the Aqueducts*.
Frontinus was Water Commissioner for Rome A.D. 97–104. In his book he described how he had improved the water supplies of Rome.

SOURCE 14

Doctors are bad for you

There is no doubt that the doctors, in their hunt for popularity by means of some new idea, did not hesitate to buy it with our lives ... Hence that gloomy inscription on monuments: 'It was the crowd of physicians [doctors] which killed me.' Medicine changes every day and we are swept along on the puffs of the clever brains of the Greek doctors – as if thousands of people do not live without doctors ...

Pliny, *Natural History*.
Pliny (A.D. 23–79) was a Roman politician, scientist and historian.

SOURCE 15

Buying loyalty

[Emperor-worship] gave clearly and frequently to the country folk the message that loyalty to Rome and loyalty to the imperial family were the same thing ...

Their devotion to the ruling family was reciprocated [paid back] by members of the imperial family. They invested directly in community improvements and encouraged the ruling elite to do the same ...

S.L. Dyson, *Society in Roman Italy*, 1992.

SOURCE 16

A place to gossip

Community interaction [socialising] also took place at the public baths. The social and sanitary roles that bathing played in Roman life are well known ... All members of Roman society frequented the baths ...

The baths were made possible by a complicated system of water supply. The provision of water played a central role in the life of these hot, dry Italian towns ...

S.L. Dyson, *Society in Roman Italy*, 1992.

SOURCE 17

Wealth and peace

The power of Rome was attended with some beneficial consequences to mankind. [These included] social life, laws, agriculture, and science ... an equal government and common language ... the increasing splendour of the cities ... and the long festival of peace.

Edward Gibbon, *The Decline and Fall of the Roman Empire*, 1776–88.

Knowledge and understanding

Use pages 7–10 to answer the following questions on the development of public health under the Greeks and Romans.

1 Who was the Father of Medicine?

2 Who was the Father of Physiology?

3 Using the diagram of the four humours (Source 9), explain the reasoning behind the different recommendations in Source 10. Explain your answers carefully.

4 Read Source 8. Identify all the factors which, according to Hippocrates, influence health. Suggest reasons why this source is seen by some historians as a turning point in the history of public health.

5 Why were Greek ideas adopted by the Romans?

6 Each of the sources on this page (Sources 12–17) suggests a reason why a large-scale public health system developed in the Roman Empire. Using these ideas, write an essay:
Why did the Romans develop a public health system?
Devote a paragraph to explaining each idea. Remember to try to:
• explain how each cause led the Romans to improve public health;
• classify each cause as 'social', 'economic', 'political', etc.;
• explain how different causes are connected;
• assess the relative importance of the different causes.

Investigation

How good was public health in Roman Britain?

Was public health in Roman Britain as good as the system in Rome? There is a great deal of information about health and medicine in the Roman Empire, but little evidence from Roman Britain survived.

SOURCE A

The Romans were the first people to plan and carry out a programme of public health on a large scale ... The Romans did more than any people before them to keep the mass of people healthy ...

Schools Council History Project, *Medicine Through Time*, 1976.

SOURCE B

[In Britain] Roman towns were provided with sewerage, drainage and water supply systems. These varied considerably from the complex underground sewers of Lincoln, into which drains from every street emptied, to the simpler wood-lined street drains of Silchester and Cirencester which emptied into pits. Most towns were provided with public water supplies by means of aqueducts ... The principal users of the water system, however, were the patrons of the public bath house, which was a key feature of every major town, not only for health and hygiene, but also as a public meeting place.

Plantagenet Somerset Fry, *Roman Britain*, 1984.

SOURCE C

At Leicester ... an ambitious aqueduct was planned to bring in water. But the surveyor got his figures wrong – the source of the water was twenty feet lower than the site of the baths ... At St Albans in the fourth century, garbage was systematically disposed of in the remains of the theatre ...

A. Birley, *Life in Roman Britain*, 1981.

SOURCE D

A Roman altar found at Chester
The inscription, which was written in Greek, read: 'To the mighty saviour gods I, Hermogenes the doctor, set up this altar.' You may be able to make out the Greek words ΕΡΜΟΓΕΝΗΣ ('Hermogenes') and IATPOC ('iatros', meaning 'doctor').

SOURCE E

Surgical instruments in Roman Britain
Back, left to right: cupping vessel used to bleed the patient (the hot vessel was placed on a scratch on the skin; as it cooled, a vacuum was created and the blood was sucked out), retractor and probe. Front, left to right: forceps, case, knife, spatula, tenaculum (hook), spoon, tweezers.

continued

SOURCE F

This reconstruction by a modern artist of the latrines at Housesteads fort on Hadrian's Wall is based on archaeological excavations. The soldiers used sponges instead of lavatory paper, rinsing them out in the stream flowing through the room.

SOURCE G

Baths at the Roman military fort at Caerleon in South Wales.

SOURCE H

Sewers beneath the legionary fortress in York

The channel is 1 metre high and almost half a metre wide. It was part of an elaborate system of sewers. Manhole covers allowed access for cleaning and maintenance. Traces of sponges have been found in the sewage deposits.

SOURCE I

A plan and artist's reconstruction of the military hospital at Housesteads, with washing area, latrine, patients' room and an operating theatre. The area marked 'Use unknown' might have been a kitchen or store. Later, the building was used as a workshop.

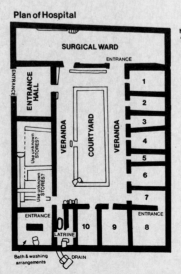

Plan of Hospital

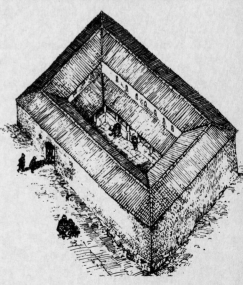

SOURCE J

A reconstruction of a Roman villa at Chedworth in Gloucestershire
The letter 'H' indicates a hypocaust (underfloor central heating) in that room.

SOURCE K

We have well over 20 prescriptions by opticians; these take the forms of inscribed small stone slabs. Thus Gaius Valerius Amandus offered 'a vinegar lotion for running eyes', 'drops for dim sight', 'poppy ointment for an attack of inflammation', as well as a mixture for clearing the sight. Other [stones] found in Chester prescribe drops, anti-irritant, ointments and saffron salve for soreness … Opticians were apparently to be found in various parts of the country, and eye troubles were prevalent. One British oculist, Stolus, became famous enough for his eye salve to be mentioned by Galen.

H.H. Scullard, *Roman Britain*, 1979.

SOURCE L

The upper classes, including all writers of memoirs and history, were not interested in [the lower classes]. Statesman looked on them merely as animals that had to be fed, in order to keep them from becoming an active danger … The crime, the crowding, the occasional suffering from starvation and pestilence, in the unfashionable quarters … these things are hidden from us, and rarely even suggested by the historians we commonly read.

W.W. Fowler, *Social Life at Rome*, 1909.

Questions

This investigation is designed to help you to decide how good a system of public health existed in Roman Britain. The first questions will ask you to form a tentative opinion; later questions will encourage you to question and refine your views.

1 Divide into groups of two or three and discuss the following:
  a What impression does Source A give of Roman public health?
  b Look at Sources B–J. Which ones support and which make you question the impression given in Source A?
  c Study Sources K and L. What questions do they raise about the nature of the evidence you have been given? Is it possible to to accept any of the sources without question?
  d Discuss whether the Romans might be said to have had a system of public health. Measure their system against the 'criteria by which you would identify whether a country has a public health system', which you established on page 4.

2 As a whole class, debate the motion: 'The Romans brought public health to Britain.'

3 Copy out Source A.
Write an essay:
How true a picture of public health in Roman Britain does Source A give?
Writing the assignment:
Your essay will evaluate a number of Roman 'achievements' – for instance, water supplies, the baths, sewage and refuse, medicine, and housing. Devote a paragraph to each issue.

You will have realised during the debate that the information in the sources can support an argument either way. Try to argue the case between the two possibilities, and come to a considered opinion.

4 Look critically at your list of criteria for identifying a public health system. Have you changed your opinions in any way after studying Chapter 1? Make any necessary changes.

The Great Failure?

The Roman Empire collapsed in the fifth century A.D. In the centuries that followed, Europe was overrun by invaders: Goths, Vandals, Huns, Anglo-Saxons, Vikings. Europe disintegrated into hundreds of tiny independent states. They did not possess the wealth or political stability to maintain an adequate public health system.

For the modern historian Charles Singer, the Middle Ages (c. 400–1500) were a time of regression and decay – the 'Great Failure'. Civilisation seemed to move backwards. Crop failures, natural disasters, famines and wars sifted the population.

Medicine in Britain in the early Middle Ages

Anglo-Saxon doctors were called leeches. They could do external surgery (operations on the outside of the body) and had a few leech houses (hospitals).

Nevertheless, Anglo-Saxon people do not appear to have possessed good health. King Alfred the Great (849–899) was in continual pain with piles and 'a severe disease unknown to the doctors'. Archaeological evidence suggests that the average height of his subjects was 1.71 metres (men) and 1.56 metres (women). We can tell from their skeletons that many people suffered from arthritis, and that their ankles were damaged from squatting round the fire (few households had chairs). War and disease helped to reduce the average lifespan. At Thetford, the men lived to about 38 years of age and the women to only 31 years. The chronicles of the period A.D. 534–1087 (553 years) record 108 years in which there was a plague, famine, animal disease or climatic disaster somewhere in the British Isles.

Much of our knowledge about life in Britain in the early Middle Ages comes from a monk who lived at Jarrow monastery in Northumbria. Bede, as we know him, was a careful historian, who checked his sources and rejected wild miracle stories. His writings allow us to deduce how Anglo-Saxon people thought about disease, doctors, health and medicine.

SOURCE 2

An Anglo-Saxon plague

[Queen Etheldreda became abbess of the convent of Ely in about A.D. 673.] Some say she not only foretold the plague that was to cause her death, but also the number of nuns who would die of it . . .

The physician Cynifid was present at her death. He used to say that during her last illness she had a large tumour under her jaw. He said, 'I was asked to open the tumour and drain away the poisonous matter in it. I did this, and for two days she seemed somewhat easier . . . But on the third day her pain returned, and she was taken from this world . . .'.

It is said that she welcomed pain of this kind, and used to say, 'I used to wear the needless burden of jewellery, and I believe that God wants me to endure this pain so that my needless vanity may be forgiven. So now I wear a burning red tumour on my neck instead of gold and pearls.'

Bede, *History of the English Church and People*, A.D. 731. One historian thinks this story refers to an outbreak of the bubonic plague. Another suggests the disease was a tuberculous swelling on the neck.

D A T A P O I N T

Anglo-Saxon leechdoms

Several Anglo-Saxon leeches left books of cures – herbal remedies, charms and prayers against all kinds of diseases. The most famous of these is the *Leechbook* of Bald, an Anglo-Saxon doctor who lived in the tenth century A.D.:

For 'theor' disease

Oxa taught this leechdom: take wallwort, cloffing, kneeholn, everlasting, cammock and tunsing-wort, nine parts, brownwort, bishopwort, attorlothe and red nettle, red hove, wormwood, yarrow, horehound, pellitory and pennyroyal. Put all these worts into Welsh or foreign ale, and then let him drink it nine days, and bleed him.

The Leechbook of Bald

theor: an inflammation or swelling
Oxa: the name of an Anglo-Saxon doctor
leechdom: a recipe for a cure
The 16 'worts' are all wild plants.

A cure for cancer

Burn a fresh dog's head to ashes, apply to the wound. If it will not yield to that, take a man's dung, dry it thoroughly, rub to dust, apply it. If with this you are not able to cure him, you may never do it by any means.

The Leechbook of Bald

Against fever disease

A man shall write this upon the communion plate, and wash it off into the drink with holy water:

+++ Λ +++++ C D +++++++++

and sing over it, In principio erat verbum etc. (John 1.1). Then wash the writing with holy water off the dish into the drink, then sing the Creed and the Lord's Prayer, and this lay: Beati Immaculati, Psalm 119 with the twelve prayer psalms. And let each of the two men [the leech and the patient] sip thrice of the water.

The Leechbook of Bald
Psalm 119 is the longest psalm in the Bible. It has 176 verses.

SOURCE 3

Lack of criticism

There is a remarkable absence of criticism at the lack of success [of Anglo-Saxon doctors] ... Perhaps this was due to the fact that illness was a general and frequent feature in Anglo-Saxon society and there was no real expectation of relief ... Another reason would possibly stem from the fact that leeches must have been relatively few in number and could only have been patronised or retained by the more wealthy.

S. Rubin, *Medieval English Medicine*, 1974.

Knowledge and understanding

Use pages 14–16 to answer the following questions about public health in Anglo-Saxon times.

1 Find examples which prove that:
a the Anglo-Saxons had certain surgical skills;
b there were doctors;
c they used herbs and natural substances;
d they used magic and religion in healing.

2 What do you think might have been the thinking behind the recommendation to recite Psalm 119 in the cure for fever?

3 Assemble all the evidence which suggests that standards of public health had fallen since Roman times.

4 What can a historian learn from Source 2 about Anglo-Saxon attitudes to disease?

5 What two reasons does Rubin suggest (Source 3) for Anglo-Saxon people's reluctance to criticise their doctors? Find evidence in this section to support his ideas. Try to think of other possible reasons.

Health and hygiene in the later Middle Ages

During the later Middle Ages (1066–1500) many books were written – for the wealthy – advising their readers about health, not only in matters of everyday personal cleanliness, but also about such things as pregnancy and childbirth.

After 1200, towns grew in size and importance. Town councils recognised that they had to take action to preserve public health. It is by no means certain that they were unhealthy places (see **Investigation: Were towns really so unhealthy?** on pages 21–23).

In Britain, town councils were not the only authority; the Church and the craft guilds (associations) were also very powerful. Both recognised their responsibility for public welfare.

The craftsmen's guilds organised sick-pay, pensions and retirement homes for their members.

Monasteries had *lavatoria* where the monks washed themselves, and infirmaries for the sick. Many of the great hospitals were founded in the later Middle Ages under the control of the Church – for instance, St Bartholomew's Hospital (St Barts) in London was founded in 1123. In 1247, Bethlehem hospital for the insane (Bedlam) was founded; in 1400 its equipment included four pairs of manacles, eleven iron chains, six locks and keys and two stocks. (On hospitals, see also page 20.)

The Black Death

Between 1347 and 1350 the Black Death ravaged Europe. Symptoms varied, but most of the sick developed black swellings (buboes) in their armpits and groin. Boils and black blotches spread over their skin. Everything about them – their breath and sweat, the blood and pus which oozed from the buboes, their urine and excrement – smelled foul. Most victims died in great pain and distress within five days.

Ignorant of germs, doctors were unable to recommend anything which would prevent or cure the disease. They told their patients not to sleep with their mouth open, to stay indoors and keep cool, to go to the stables to be breathed on by the horses, or even to spend hours sitting in the sewers. The suspicion that the disease was caused by a miasma (poisonous vapours), perhaps caused by earthquakes, led doctors to tell their patients to fill their houses

SOURCE 4

Lepers
People with leprosy were forced to live in specially built lazar houses, named after the parable of Lazarus in the Bible (Luke, Chapter 16). They had to wear distinctive dress, and to carry a bell. As a result, leprosy largely died out in England during the later Middle Ages – 'the first great success of preventative medicine'.
This picture shows lepers in Paris in the 14th century. One of the lepers carries a begging bowl and a rattle.

with pleasant smells by burning juniper and oak. As some doctors blamed deadly winds from the equator, houses were built with no windows on the south side. Doctors who believed that the disease was caused by an imbalance of the humours prescribed purgatives and bleeding. Others gave dietary advice, telling their patients to avoid meat, milk and fish, and to eat bread, fruit, eggs, vegetables and nuts (figs and rue were best before breakfast, and myrrh and pepper were better later in the day).

Some cures did more harm than good; doctors prescribed theriac (a potion which included parts of chopped-up snakes that had been dead for ten years), and pills made from ingredients such as ten-year-old treacle, arsenic and crushed emeralds.

In London, more practically, Edward III ordered the Lord Mayor to clean up the city (**Source 5**).

The Black Death carried off perhaps a third of the population. 'The doctors were useless and indeed shameful, as they dared not visit the sick for fear of becoming infected,' admitted Guy de Chauliac, the Pope's doctor. Many people simply fled, carrying the disease to other cities. Others retreated into superstition and despair. In some places 'men walked about as if mad', and in others bands of flagellants whipped themselves to try to earn God's forgiveness. Town government collapsed; in many places it was said that there were not enough left alive to bury the dead. 'People said and believed, "This is the end of the world",' wrote one Italian chronicler.

SOURCE 5

6 April, Langley Castle

Order to cause the human faeces and other filth lying in the streets ... to be removed with all speed ... and to cause the city to be cleaned ... so that no greater cause of mortality may arise from such smells.

The King has learned how the city ... is so foul with the filth from out of the houses by day and night that the air is infected and the city poisoned to the danger of men ... especially by the contagious sickness which increases daily.

Calendar of Close Rolls, 1349.
faeces: excrement
mortality: death
There is no evidence that this order had any effect on the cleanliness of the town.

Ideas about medicine in the later Middle Ages

Some historians claim that there was a gradual improvement in surgery during the Middle Ages. Nevertheless, there is a great deal of evidence dating from towards the end of the period which shows that medieval medicine was often unsuccessful, and that doctors had become very unpopular. The sources on these pages will allow you to form your own opinion about medicine in the later Middle Ages.

SOURCE A

Blood-letting

It contains the beginning of health. It concentrates the mind, aids the memory, clears the brain, reforms the bladder, warms the bones, improves the hearing, checks tears, removes nausea, benefits the stomach, aids digestion, strengthens the voice, moves the bowels, enriches sleep, removes anxiety, and nourishes good health.

French manuscript, 12th century.

SOURCE C

Surgery for piles *c.* 1200
Notice the word *emoroida* (haemorrhoids), the doctor's knife and the bowl to catch the blood.

SOURCE B

Surgery for epilepsy *c.* 1200
A surgeon opens the skull to release the demon. Surgeons used wine (a mild antiseptic) to clean wounds, and mandrake and opium to dull the pain. They could perform successful operations for cataracts, bladder stones, facial ulcers, hare lip and nasal polyps.

SOURCE D

A sick woman and her doctor in the 13th century
The doctor has made a diagnosis after studying his patient's urine. He drops the urine flask to indicate that she is going to die.

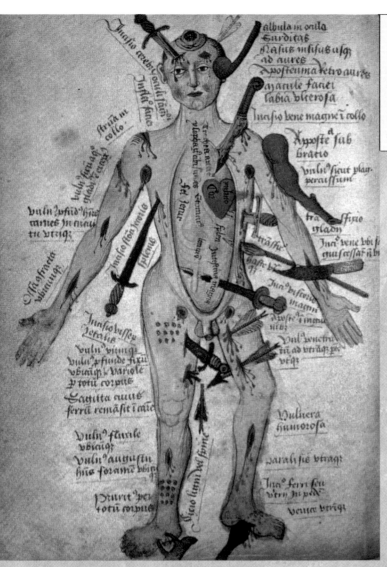

Wound Man in the 14th century
Diagrams such as these were, in fact, advertisements designed to attract customers. In most cases, medieval surgeons cauterised the injury: they poured hot oil into the wound, or burned it with a red-hot cautery iron, to sterilise it and stop the bleeding.

SOURCE H

The 'perfect' physician

The cause of every malady you'd got
He knew, and whether dry, cold, moist, or hot;
He knew their seat, their humour and condition.
He was a perfect practising physician.
These causes being known for what they were,
He gave the man his medicine then and there.
All his apothecaries in a tribe
Were ready with the drugs he would prescribe
And each made money from the other's guile;
They had been friendly for a goodish while.
He was well versed in Aesculapius too
And what Hippocrates and Rufus knew …

In blood-red garments, slashed with bluish-grey
And lined with taffeta, he rode his way;
Yet he was rather close as to expenses
And kept the gold he won in pestilences.
Gold stimulates the heart, or so we're told.
He therefore had a special love of gold.

Geoffrey Chaucer, *The Canterbury Tales*, c. 1387,
translated into modern English by N. Coghill.

malady: illness
apothecaries: men who made and dispensed medicines
guile: trickery
Aesculapius: the Greek god of medicine
Rufus: a Greek doctor who lived *c.* A.D. 100
taffeta: expensive cloth of silk and linen
pestilences: epidemics

SOURCE F

To cure consumption

Here is a bath which has proved to be of value. Take blind puppies, remove the entrails, and cut off the extremities; then boil in water, and in this water let the patient be bathed: let him enter the bath for four hours after his food …
Another bath of which the patient may avail himself: Take land-tortoises, and boil them in a cooking-pot …

Johannes de Mirfield, *Breviarium Batholomei*, c. 1393.

SOURCE G

A negligent barber-surgeon

A judicial investigation between Isabel Cummay of London and John atte Hethe of London, barber … The said John … undertook … well and sufficiently to extract a certain tooth of the said Isabel, and the said John so negligently and carelessly performed the same that the jaw of the said Isabel was broken and the life of the said Isabel was despaired of.

Coram Rege Roll, 1398.
Many doctors thought surgery was degrading and left it to barber-surgeons, who did hair-cutting and tooth-pulling as well as surgery.

Questions

1 Does Source E prove that surgeons in the later Middle Ages were skilled in the treatment of wounds? Explain your answer.

2 Does Source G prove that all barber-surgeons in the later Middle Ages were incompetent? Explain your answer.

3 What evidence can you find in the sources that in the later Middle Ages doctors accepted Graeco-Roman ideas about medicine?

4 Find all the words and phrases in Source H which show that Chaucer disliked doctors. Explain your choices. Why did he dislike them?

5 Compare Anglo-Saxon and later medieval medicine. Had doctors made any progress since Anglo-Saxon times?

Hospitals in the later Middle Ages

Very few hospitals, had resident doctors, or were ever visited by doctors. Of 1103 'hospitals' in later medieval Britain, 345 were lazar houses, and 742 were almshouses for the poor, which might refuse to take in sick poor people. The hospital of St John, Bridgewater, was typical (**Source 6**).

SOURCE 6

Hospital rules

No lepers, lunatics, or persons having the falling sickness or other contagious disease, and no pregnant women, or sucking infants, and no intolerable persons, even though they be poor and infirm, may be admitted to this house, and if any be admitted by mistake, they are to be expelled as soon as possible. And when the other poor and infirm persons have recovered they are to be put out without delay.

Register of Thomas Bekynton, Bishop of Bath and Wells (1443–65).

Knowledge and understanding

Use everything you have learned from Chapter 2 (including the **Investigation: Were towns really so unhealthy?** on pages 21–23) to answer the following questions, which will help you to decide whether Charles Singer was correct when he called the Middle Ages the 'Great Failure'.

1 List the public health measures taken by:
 a the Church;
 b the guilds.

2 First, write a paragraph 'proving' that 'the Middle Ages saw the development of the first hospitals'. Then write a second paragraph 'proving' that 'hospitals, as we know them, did not exist in the Middle Ages'.

3 List the different remedies suggested by doctors against the Black Death. For each, try to suggest the thinking behind the cure.

4 List the different ways people reacted to the Black Death.

5 How did later medieval government deal with leprosy?

6 Throughout history, Christianity has had two reactions to poverty and disease. One is to pity the victims, and to try to help them. The other reaction is to assume that, as misfortune comes from God, the victims are to blame for their condition. Find examples of both attitudes in the way the sick were treated in the later Middle Ages.

7 Discuss as a whole class whether Charles Singer's description of the Middle Ages as the 'Great Failure' is justified.

SOURCE 7

A hospital in the later Middle Ages
To what extent does the artist's painting agree with what we know about hospitals in the later Middle Ages? Does this mean that it is useless as a source?

Were towns really so unhealthy?

SOURCE A

A modern drawing (1969) of a medieval town by artist Norman Meredith.

SOURCE B

The streets often had open sewers running down the middle of them. These sewers became clogged with rubbish and excrement thrown from the windows. Pigs, dogs and rats often roamed through the streets. Towns such as London sometimes tried to clean up the streets, but not very often. People had no idea that dirty conditions could lead to disease.

L. Hartley, *History of Medicine*, 1984.

SOURCE C

Archaeology reveals that [in twelfth-century England] bishops' and merchants' townhouses boasted lead pipes and stone drains ... Latrines were often neatly lined in wood or stone, periodically cleaned out, and carefully dug some distance from property boundaries ... A twelfth-century wooden toilet seat, latrine pit, and wicker screen for privacy were recently excavated in York... Peasant and burgher houses were often swept quite clean, betraying none of the litter so often ascribed to them and so regularly uncovered on late Roman sites.

E.J. Kealey, *Medieval Medicus*, 1981.

SOURCE D

Next case [heard before the wardmen of the city of London]: the lane called Ebbegate ... was a right of way for all men until it was blocked by Thomas at Wytte and William de Hockele, who got together and built latrines which stuck out from the walls of the houses. From these latrines human filth falls on the heads of the passers-by.

Book of Customs, 1321.

SOURCE E

ITEM, for that so much dung and filth of the garbage and entrails be cast and put in ditches, rivers, and other waters ... so that the air there is grown greatly corrupt and infected, and many maladies and other intolerable diseases do daily happen ... it is accorded and assented, that the proclamation be made as well in the city of London, as in other cities, boroughs, and towns through the realm of England, where it shall be needful, that all they who do cast and lay all such annoyances, dung, garbages, entrails, and other ordure, in ditches, rivers, waters, and other places aforesaid, shall cause them utterly to be removed, avoided, and carried away, every one upon pain to lose and forfeit to our Lord the King, [£20].

Parliamentary Statutes, 1388.
The first national Town Sanitation Law.

continued

SOURCE F

Monks in a stewe
Public baths (stewes) were common in late medieval towns. It was thought that baths had curative powers; sick people might take up to 40 baths a day.

Many stewes were the haunts of prostitutes – places for 'lewd men and women of bad and evil life'. Why is this picture particularly scandalous?

SOURCE G

Avoid all four stinks – the stable, stinking fields, ways for streets, dead flesh ... and most stinking waters. Just as the heart and spirits are lifted by the sweet smell of balm, so evil smells make them weak.

Bishop of Aarhus, *A Passying Gode Lityll Boke ... agenst the Pestilence*, 1485.

SOURCE J

A detail from Pieter Brueghel's painting *Children's Games* (15th century).

SOURCE H

On every side [town corporations] set up stately crosses in the market-place or provided new water-supply for the growing population ... To take a single instance, in 1421 the water-supply of Southampton was undertaken by the council, and new lead pipes provided by the grant of a burgess who had bequeathed his money 'for the good of his soul'. An aqueduct was made at considerable expense in 1428; [it took] 261 days' work [and was made of] great stones called 'scaplyd stonys', with loads of chalk, quicklime, pitch, resin, solder, wax and wood. In 1490 a new well was made with a 'watering-place for horses and a washing-place for women'.

Mrs J.R. Green, *Town Life in the Fifteenth Century*, 1894.

SOURCE I

Almost all the floors are of clay and rushes from the marshes, so carelessly renewed that the foundation sometimes remains for twenty years, harbouring there below, spittle and vomit and urine of dogs and men, beer that hath been cast forth, remnants of fishes and filth unnamable ... It would help also if ... public opinion required of the officials that the streets should be less defiled with filth and urine.

Letter from Erasmus to Peter, Cardinal Wolsey's doctor, 1524.
Erasmus was a Dutch philosopher. Cardinal Wolsey was the Chancellor of England. Erasmus was suggesting ways to prevent the epidemics of the sleeping sickness.

SOURCE K

This illustration from the Bennick Book of Hours shows an imaginary town scene in the later Middle Ages.

SOURCE L

It appears to be a general assumption that hygiene in the Middle Ages was almost non-existent. Much has been made of the various statutes and decrees from civic councils concerning the filth and refuse in the streets, squares, rivers and so forth. But it seems to have escaped attention that these are decrees which forbid the fouling of towns and cities. The conclusion to be drawn should be exactly the opposite to the one usually made.

C.H. Talbot, *Medicine in Medieval England*, 1967.

Questions

1 Read Source B. In what ways does it agree with Source A?

2 Source B makes seven statements; what are they? Divide the statements into facts and opinions.

3 In Source B, Hartley suggests a reason why people behaved in an unhealthy way. What reason does he suggest? Explain in your own words how this would have led people to behave in an unhealthy way.

4 Hartley's opinion is that medieval public health was poor . Divide into small groups of two or three. Study Sources C–K in turn. Decide for each whether it supports or contradicts Hartley's opinion. Keep a record of your decisions.

5 Distinguish between the primary sources (from the time) and the secondary sources (written or drawn many years later). Identify a primary source which would be cited:
- by a historian who wanted to prove that public health was poor in late medieval towns;
- by a historian who wanted to prove that public health was good in late medieval towns;
- by both.

6 Now read Source L. Make sure you understand what it is saying. Go through your list of those sources which seemed to support Hartley's opinion. Do you want to change any of your decisions?

7 Write an essay:
How true a picture of public health in late medieval Britain does Norman Meredith's drawing (Source A) give?
Writing the assignment:
Take the same 'achievements' that you listed for the Romans in Chapter 1 (water supplies, the baths, sewage and refuse, medicine, and housing).
Devote a paragraph to each issue. You will have realised that the information in the sources can support an argument either way. Try to argue the case between the two possibilities, and come to a considered opinion.

8 As a whole class, debate: 'Which was better: Roman public health, or medieval public health?'

'Lord, Have Mercy Upon Us'

The period from about 1450 to 1700 is called by historians the 'Early Modern Age'. It was a time of progress. The fifteenth and sixteenth centuries were the time of Renaissance (meaning 'rebirth') and Reformation (meaning 'change for the better'). The end of the seventeenth century saw the beginning of the Scientific Revolution. This chapter examines the extent to which these advances led to improvements in the health of the people.

The Great Plague

According to the Bills of Mortality (the weekly lists of deaths, see **Source 2**), the bubonic plague of 1665 killed around three to five thousand people every week, at a time when the population of London was about five hundred thousand. In the third week of September, 7165 people died. The disease, which began in the slums, was known as the 'poore's plague', on account of the large numbers of poor people who died. In May 1666, the Lord Mayor issued orders for dealing with the disease (**Source 1**).

Abortive	4	Imposthume	8	
Aged	45	Infants	22	
Bleeding	1	Kingfevil	4	
Broken legge	1	Lethargy	1	
Broke her fcull by a fall in the ftreet at St. Mary VVoolchurch	1	Livergrown	1	
		Meagrome	1	
		Palfie	1	
Childbed	28	Plague	4237	
Chrifomes	9	Purples	2	
Confumption	126	Quinfie	5	
Convulfion	89	Rickets	23	
Cough	1	Rifing of the Lights	18	
Dropfie	53	Rupture	1	
Feaver	348	Scurvy	3	
Flox and Small-pox	11	Shingles	1	
Flux	1	Spotted Feaver	166	
Frighted	2	Stilborn	4	
Gowt	1	Stone	2	
Grief	3	Stopping of the ftomach	17	
Griping in the Guts	79	Strangury	3	
Head-mould-fhot	1	Suddenly	2	
Jaundies	7	Surfeit	74	
		Teeth	111	
		Thrufh	6	
		Tiffick	9	
		Ulcer	1	
		Vomiting	10	
		Winde	4	
		Wormes	20	

Chriftned { Males — 90 Females — 81 In all — 171 } Buried { Males — 2777 Females — 2791 In all — 5568 } Plague — 4237

Increafed in the Burials this Week — 249
Parifhes clear of the Plague — 27 Parifhes Infected — 103

The Affize of Bread fet forth by Order of the Lord Maior and Coors of Aldermen, A penny Wheaten Loaf to contain Nine Ounces and a half, and three half-penny White Loaves the like weight.

SOURCE 2

A Bill of Mortality
The Bills were compiled by female searchers 'of honest reputation' appointed in every parish. How accurate do you think they would have been?

Chrisomes: deaths of infants under one month old
Consumption: tuberculosis
Dropsie: water collecting in the tissues of the body
Flux: dysentery
Head-mould-shot: the bones of the skull overlap each other
Imposthume: abscess
Kingsevil: scrofula (a form of tuberculosis)
Lights: lungs
Livergrown: enlarged liver
Meagrome: migraine headache

Palsie: paralysis or weakness of the limbs
Plurisie: pleurisy; water on the lungs
Purples: livid red spots or buboes
Quinsie: a form of tonsilitis
Rickets: softening of the bones and deformity, usually in children
Scurvy: a disease of malnutrition, caused by lack of fresh vegetables and fruit
Strangury: difficult and painful urination
Surfeit: overeating
Thrush: sore mouth and throat
Tissick: lung disease, either asthma, or tuberculosis

SOURCE 1

Keeping the streets clean

It is ordered that every Householder do cause the Street to be daily prepared before his Door, and so to keep it clean swept all the Week long … That no Hogs, Dogs, or Cats, or tame Pigeons, or Conies [rabbits], to be kept within any part of the City, or any Swine stray in the Streets or Lanes, and that the Dogs be killed by the Dog-killers.

Orders published by the Lord Mayor, 1666.
However, no action was taken against the rats, which carried the fleas which spread the plague!

Early Modern medicine

> Although the conditions of the towns and the houses of the poor remained little changed since medieval times (see **Investigation: Were towns really so unhealthy?** on pages 21–23), medical knowledge did improve.

Some of the advances of the Early Modern Age were of major importance. In the sixteenth century Andreas Vesalius (1514–64), an Italian professor, greatly improved the knowledge of the anatomy of the human body (**Sources 4** and **5**. In 1628 the English doctor William Harvey (1578–1657) discovered the circulation of the blood. The invention of the microscope in 1590 allowed doctors to study the body in great detail; in 1683 a Dutchman called Antonie van Leeuwenhoek (1632–1723) discovered and drew tiny creatures (bacteria) which he had found in the human mouth. In 1796 the English doctor Edward Jenner began vaccinating people against smallpox by infecting them with cowpox (**Source 6**). Cowpox is a similar but not fatal disease; when the body defences have learned to cope with cowpox, they can also cope with smallpox. Jenner did not have a clue why his discovery worked, but it was the beginning of a process which by 1980 had made the smallpox germ extinct.

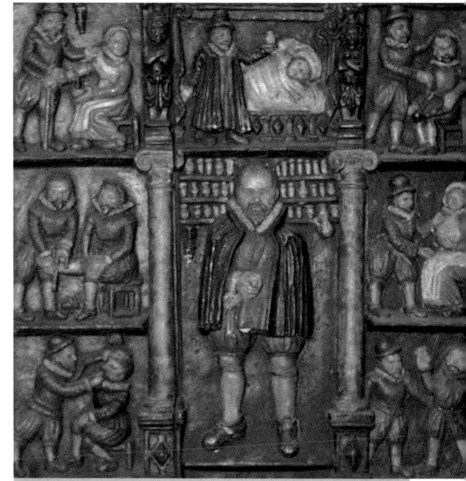

SOURCE 3

17th century physician
The painted wooden signboard, dated 1623, of a physician from Poole, Dorsetshire. In the centre, he stands in front of shelves of drugs. His business includes (clockwise from bottom left): extracting a tooth, amputating a leg, bleeding a patient, diagnosing illness by examining the patient's urine, correcting a dislocated shoulder, cauterising a breast tumour and examining a man with a paralysed arm.

SOURCES 4 AND 5

Illustrations from (left) the *Margarita Philosophica* of Gregory Reisch, 1503, and (right) Andreas Vesalius' book, *The Fabric of the Human Body*, 1543.

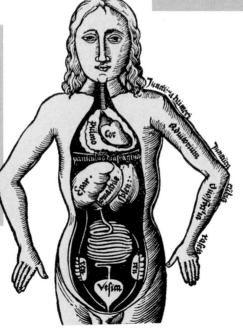

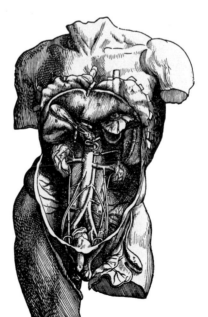

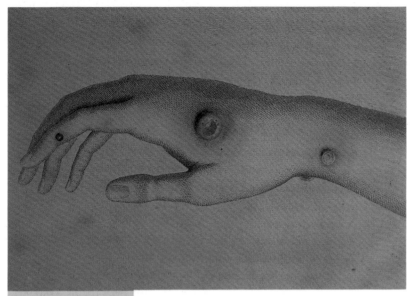

SOURCE 6

Cowpox
Jenner's drawing of cowpox pustules on the hand of a milkmaid called Sarah Nelmes. People who had been infected with cowpox did not get smallpox. As the Latin word for cow is *vacca*, one of Jenner's friends called the procedure 'vaccination'.

Advances in knowledge about the body, however, did not lead to improved health. Doctors continued to use magic and primitive methods of healing (see **Sources 3, 7, 8** and **9**). According to the modern historian Peter Laslett, the average lifespan during the Early Modern Age fell from 38 years in 1601, to 36 years in 1661, and to 32.5 years in 1721.

Much more important for the long-term improvement of the nation's health was the beginning of a state system of poor relief in England after 1597. In 1688 the statistician Gregory King estimated that the government spent £600,000 a year on poor relief. By 1831 the nation was spending over £7 million per annum on poor relief to help to support over a million paupers (ten per cent of the population).

SOURCE 7

1 January 1717

I am now confined to the house and have daily three dismal visitors – the Doctor, the Apothecary and the Surgeon. The first prescribes, the second prepares and administers for my complaints of head and stomach; the third has bin near a month in hand with a hot fiery toe where there was a swelling. He has raised the nail and cut half away, root and all … and has every day since ply'd me oft with his crook-shanked sheers, lancet and incision knives, besides his fiery oyles and burning powders …

Letter from Sir Henry Liddell to a friend.

SOURCE 8

For a mad dog's bite

Of ye leaves of Rue pick'd from ye Stalks, six ounces, garlic pick'd and bruis'd four ounces, Venice treacle four ounces, scrapings of Pewter four ounces. Boil these ingredients over a slow fire in 2 quarts of strong Ale till one Pinte is [boiled away]; then keep it in a Bottle close stop'd and give of it 7 spoonfuls to a man or woman, warm, seven mornings fasting, and six to a dog. This the author believes will not by God's blessing fail, if it be given within 9 days after ye bite of ye dog.

From an eighteenth-century diary.
Rue: a herb
Pewter: a metal from which plates and mugs were made

Knowledge and understanding

Use all the information in this chapter to answer the following questions about the extent to which increases in medical knowledge led to improvements in treatment and health in the sixteenth and seventeenth centuries.

1 Study Source 2. Discuss the similarities and differences between the diseases of people in the seventeenth century and today.

2 Compare Sources 4 and 5. What improvements in the knowledge of anatomy do they reveal?

3 Find examples to prove that Early Modern doctors:
a had surgical ability;
b used herbs and natural substances;
c used magic and religion in healing.

4 Compare Source 3 with your knowledge of medieval doctors (see Chapter 2). Had doctors progressed since medieval times?

5 Why did the discoveries made by doctors in the Early Modern Age not lead to improvements in the way doctors treated patients? Think of as many reasons as you can. Try to find evidence in this chapter to support your ideas.

6 Copy out what is, in your opinion, the most important fact about Thomas Sydenham in the Datapoint on page 27.

SOURCE 9

Even in the 17th century, astrology and magic played a part in medicine. Here an alchemist seeks to discover the 'philosopher's stone' that would turn lead into gold and give the secret of eternal life.

D A T A P O I N T

Thomas Sydenham

Thomas Sydenham, a London physician, was known as 'the English Hippocrates'. Sydenham:

- studied at the universities of Oxford and Montpellier (in France);
- wrote only two small books, *Medical Observations* and *A Treatise on the Gout* (from which he suffered himself);
- rejected book-learning, and recommended instead careful observation of the patient, and the keeping of case histories of the disease and the weather;
- rejected the idea that disease was spread by contagion;
- claimed that disease was the result of combinations of circumstances he called 'constitutions'. 'Atmospheric constitutions' (the weather and climate, heat and moisture) caused diseases such as fever and pleurisy. 'Environmental constitutions' (including 'emanations' from the soil) caused diseases such as the plague;
- accepted the theory of the four humours as the explanation for many diseases (for instance, gout);
- recommended bleeding, sweating, purging and drugs such as opium, quinine (for malaria) and mercury (for syphilis) to cure diseases;
- urged doctors to leave the microscope, dissection and 'counting and measuring', and to seek cures instead;
- was a supporter of Oliver Cromwell, which meant that his ideas were rejected in his own time, and he never became one of the king's doctors or a fellow of the Royal College of Physicians.

SOURCE 10

Thomas Sydenham
(1624–89)

A journal of the plague year

SOURCE A

The face of London was now indeed strangely altered ... It was a most surprising thing to see the streets which were usually so thronged now grown desolate. I went up to Holborn, and there the street was full of people, but they walked in the middle of the great street, because, as I suppose, they would not mingle with anybody that came out of the houses, or meet with smells and scents from houses that might be infected. Whole rows of houses in some places were shut close up, the inhabitants all fled, and only a watchman or two left ...

The Government appointed public prayers and days of fasting and humiliation, to make public confession of sin and implore the mercy of God to avert the dreadful judgement which hung over their heads; and the public showed that they would bear their share in these things. All the plays were forbid to act; the gaming-tables, public dancing-rooms and music-houses, which multiplied and began to debauch [corrupt] the manners of the people, were shut up and suppressed; for the minds of the people were agitated with other things. Death was before their eyes, and everybody began to think of their graves, not of mirth and divertion.

The magistrates began to take the condition of the people into their serious consideration. As to the affair of health, having seen the foolish humour of the people in running after quacks, wizards and fortune-tellers, which they did even to madness, the Lord Mayor, a very sober and religious gentleman, appointed physicians and surgeons for the relief of the poor – I mean the diseased poor – and in particular ordered the College of Physicians to publish directions for cheap remedies for the poor....

The Justices of the Peace had begun to shut up houses, and it was with good success; for in several streets where the plague broke out, upon strict guarding the houses that were infected, and taking care to bury the dead immediately after they were known to be dead, the plague ceased in those streets. The shutting up of houses was at first counted a very cruel and unchristian method, and complaints of the severity of it were daily brought to my Lord Mayor, of houses causelessly (and some maliciously) shut up. It was a public good that justified the private mischief ... but the misery of those families is not to be expressed; and it was generally in such houses that we heard the most dismal shrieks and outcries of the poor people, terrified and even frightened to death by the sight of the condition of their dearest relatives, and by the terror of being imprisoned as they were.

I went all the first part of the time freely about the streets, though not so freely as to run myself into danger, except when they dug the great pit in the churchyard of our parish of Aldgate. A terrible pit it was, and I could not resist my curiosity to go and see it. As near as I may judge, it was about forty feet in length and about fifteen or sixteen feet broad, and at the time I first looked at it, about nine feet deep; but it was said that they dug it near twenty feet deep afterwards. Because of the order of the magistrates confining them to leave no bodies within six feet of the surface, the pit being finished the 4th of September, I think, by the 20th they had thrown into it 1,114 bodies, when they were obliged to fill it up, the bodies being then come to lie within six feet of the surface.

The distemper was, indeed, very horrible in itself. The swellings, which were generally in the neck or groin, when they grew hard and would not break, grew so painful that it was equal to the most exquisite torture; and some, not able to bear the torture, threw themselves out at windows or shot themselves. Others, unable to contain themselves, vented their pain by incessant roarings. Dr Heath coming to visit me, and finding that I ventured so often out in the streets, earnestly persuaded me to lock myself in and my family, and not to suffer any of us to go out of doors; to keep all our windows fast, shutters and curtains closed, and never to open them; but first, to make a very strong smoke in the room where the window or door was to be opened, with resin and pitch, brimstone or gunpowder and the like.

However, the poor people could not lay up provisions, and there was a necessity that they must go to market to buy; and as this brought abundance of unsound people to the markets, a great many that went there sound brought death home with them. It is true people used all possible precaution. When anyone bought a joint of meat in the market, they would not take it off the butcher's hands, but took it off the hooks themselves. On the other hand, the butcher would not touch the money, but have it put into a pot full of vinegar. They carried bottles of scents and perfumes in their hands; but then the poor could not do even these things, and they went at all hazards.

The work of removing the dead bodies by carts was now grown very odious and dangerous, for innumerable of the bearers died of the distemper, infected by the bodies they were obliged to come so near. And had it not been that the number of poor people who wanted employment and wanted bread was so great that necessity drove them to undertake anything and venture anything, they would never have found people to be employed. But the magistrates cannot be enough commended in this, that they kept such good order for the burying of the dead, that notwithstanding the infinite number of people which died and were sick, almost all together, yet they were always cleared away and carried off every night, so that it was never said of London that the living were not able to bury the dead.

The magistrates wisely made very good bye-laws for regulating citizens and keeping good order in the streets. In the first place the Lord Mayor and sheriffs came to a resolution and published it, viz., that they would not quit the city themselves, but would always be at hand for preserving good order in every place; and all manner of presumptuous rogues, such as thieves, housebreakers, plunderers of the dead or of the sick, were duly

SOURCE B

A scene from a plague poster
The doors of the houses are marked with red crosses; outside stand armed guards. To the left are two searchers; each carries a staff to indicate her authority. Two men are killing the dogs. A fire burns outside every sixth house to 'purify the air'.

punished. Also constables and churchwardens were enjoined to stay in the city upon severe penalties. These things re-established the minds of the people very much. Also the bakers were taken under particular order, and were obliged to keep their ovens going constantly, on pain of losing the priviliges of a freeman of the city of London.

It is to be observed that while the plague continued so violent in London, two particular trades were carried on by water-carriage all the while of the infection, very much to the advantage and comfort of the poor distressed people of the city, and those were the coasting trade for corn, and the Newcastle trade for coals. This was also, much of it, owing to the prudence and conduct of the Lord Mayor, who took such care to keep the masters and seamen from danger when they came up, and ordered the coal ships not to come up into the Pool above a certain number at a time.

However, it pleased God, by the continuing of the winter weather, so to restore the health of the city that by the February following we reckoned the distemper quite ceased. It was a common thing to meet people in the streets that were strangers … expressing their surprise. Going one day through Aldgate, a man said, I heard him, "Tis all wonderful; 'tis all a dream.' 'Blessed be God,' says another man. I can go no farther here. I shall conclude the account of this calamitous year with my own coarse stanza, which I placed at the end of my ordinary memorandums the same year they were written:

A dreadful plague in London was
In the year sixty-five,
Which swept an hundred-thousand souls
Away; yet I alive!

Daniel Defoe, *A Journal of the Plague Year*, 1722.

Questions

Divide into pairs. Read together the extract from *A Journal of the Plague Year*.

1 What evidence can you find that the people of the time thought bad smells caused disease?

2 Make a list of those responses to the plague which might be listed under the heading: 'Religion and superstition'.

3 List the actions taken by the authorities against the plague. Discuss whether this is 'public health'

4 List the responses (including the attitudes and actions) of the following groups of people to the plague:
  • the author of the journal;
  • the doctors;
  • the poor.

5 Using your answers to Questions 1–4, compare the impact of the plague in 1665 with its effect in 1348–49 (see pages 16–17). How much had things improved?

6 Daniel Defoe, the author, was not an eye-witness! He was only six in 1665, and wrote his book 57 years later, when the plague had broken out in Portugal and it was feared that it would again spread to London. Defoe's book was a piece of propaganda designed to frighten the authorities into making adequate preparations. To what extent does this reduce the value of Defoe's account? Where might he have got his information?

4 The Sanitary Revolution

SOURCE 1

'Night'
A street scene by
William Hogarth
(1697–1764).
The barber-surgeon's
sign reads: 'Shaving,
bleeding and teeth
drawn with a touch.'

Historical change does not occur suddenly, nor does it have one cause. It is usually the result of a combination of many different factors, which may take centuries to come together. Historians call these factors 'preconditions'. There were great improvements in public health during the Industrial Revolution of the nineteenth century (see pages 36–41). These changes, however, had their roots in developments which occurred in the eighteenth century.

In this section you will study the developing preconditions which produced the public health system of nineteenth-century Britain. Historians have identified the following as being most important:

* reasons for the government to act;
* a society which is sufficiently wealthy and organised;
* a technology sufficiently advanced to allow improvements in health;
* a theory of disease and public attitudes which encourage action;
* influential individuals.

The miasma theory of disease

In the eighteenth century the idea became accepted throughout Europe that disease was caused by poisonous vapours and airborne particles. These were called miasmas (sometimes emanations or effluvia). The Scottish writer John Arbuthnot explained the causes of the flu epidemic of 1732–33 like this:

> Both before and during the Continuance of the Disease in *England*, the Air was warm, with great Quantities of sulphureous Vapours ... The Earth had emitted several new Effluvia hurtful to Human Bodies; this appear'd to be the Case by the thick and stinking Fogs ...
>
> J. Arbuthnot, *Essay Concerning the Effects of Air on Human Bodies*, 1733.

Arbuthnot, like most eighteenth-century doctors, claimed to have taken his ideas from Thomas Sydenham (see page 27). The modern historian J.C. Riley thinks that this was mainly due to a successful advertising campaign after Sydenham's death, when the English writer John Locke had written to doctors all over Europe, publicising 'the esteeme which Phisitians [doctors] have had of Doctor Sydenham and his books'. Writers of the time preferred to ascribe their theories to an accepted expert rather than declare them as their own; so Sydenham was accredited with ideas he had never had!

All over Europe doctors experimented and collected facts about the miasmas which they believed caused disease. In Italy a doctor called Gattoni tied up little boys in leather bags and plunged them into warm water to make them break wind, to test whether bowel odours were harmful to health. In Paris, in 1790, two French doctors walked through the city noting every smell over a distance of 10 kilometres.

The miasma theory was wrong – bad smells do *not* cause illness! Yet it is a remarkable fact that this belief led to genuine improvements in public health more than a century *before* Louis Pasteur discovered (in 1864) that bacteria cause disease.

Some of the first changes were introduced by the armed forces (it is interesting to compare this with Roman public health, see pages 9–10). In 1752 John Pringle, an army doctor, published his *Observations on the Diseases of the Army*, and in 1757 James Lind published an *Essay on the Most Effectual Means of Preserving the Health of Seamen*. Both men recommended ventilation, cleanliness, fresh water, and proper food and clothing. On his voyage to Australia, Captain Cook fanatically followed their advice; hammocks and sails were brought up on deck to air, and every package was regularly untied to let any miasmas disperse. Cook ordered rotten food to be thrown out and kept the crew clear of smells from the cargo; during the voyage, the cargo hatches were firmly closed and completely sealed with tar. His ship was the healthiest in the fleet.

Knowledge and understanding

Use pages 31–32 to answer the following questions.

1 What books were written by:
a John Pringle? **b** James Lind?

2 What happened in towns that had obtained an Improvement Act from parliament?

3 Why is 1795 an important date in the history of public health?

4 Explain the miasma theory of the cause of disease.

5 Explain the following, in the light of the miasma theory:
a Arbuthnot's description of the flu epidemic of 1732–33;
b Pringle's actions at Newgate Gaol in 1750;
c Cook's health precautions on his voyage to Australia in 1768–71.

6 List the health hazards you can see in Hogarth's engraving of *Night* (Source 1). In the light of the miasma theory, which of these would have been thought most dangerous to health by eighteenth-century doctors?

7 Explain why the miasma theory was important in the development of public health in the eighteenth century, even though it was incorrect.

8 Reread the **Datapoint: Thomas Sydenham** (see page 27). In the light of your answers to Questions 5–7, which fact about Sydenham now seems the most important?

Such ideas also spread to the prisons. In 1750 Pringle had been asked for his advice after 'gaol fever' (probably typhus) had killed not only some of the prisoners of Newgate Gaol, but also two judges and the Lord Mayor of London. Pringle employed builders to install ventilators, and the prisoners' health improved. When the family of one of the workmen caught the fever, Pringle declared that it was due to the man's 'remarkably offensive' breath, sweat and excrement.

It was soon realised that towns also were smelly – and therefore unhealthy – places. Towns such as York applied to parliament for Improvement Acts. They paved and widened the roads and built sewers; the death rate dropped noticeably. Local swamps were drained to reduce the incidence of malaria (the word *malaria* means bad air). Then in 1795 a group of doctors formed the Manchester Board of Health. As well as improving the sanitation of the town, it forbade mill-owners to employ children as apprentices for more than ten hours a day.

It is important to remember that the miasma theory was the theoretical basis for all the public health measures taken before 1864.

The coming of public health

Today, we would find the pace of change during the early years of the Industrial Revolution impossibly slow. At the time, it took Britain completely by surprise. Even in towns which had obtained Improvement Acts (see above), the growth of industry and population overwhelmed the powers of the local councils (**Source 2**).

Few rich people ever visited poor areas, and most believed that their success was due to their own ability and effort. The poor at the base of society were therefore thought to be failures – people to

SOURCE 2

Life expectancy in 1842

Class	Leeds	Liverpool	Manchester	Rutlandshire
Professional persons and the gentry	44	35	38	52
Farmers and tradesmen	27	22	20	41
Labourers and craftsmen	19	15	17	38

Report on the Sanitary Condition of the Labouring Population of Great Britain, 1842. Rutlandshire was a country area. It was included to provide a comparison with the terrible conditions in the towns.

be criticised (see the last paragraph of **Source 4** on page 36). Early Victorians believed the Bible, which said: 'The poor shall never cease out of the land'; their problems could therefore be dismissed with a fatalistic shrug of the shoulders. The accepted principle was one of *laissez faire* (let things be).

Yet at a time when the poor were thought to be to blame for their own poverty and ratepayers objected to paying poor rates, when the government believed that it should not intervene in the lives of its citizens, and before the discovery of germs, Britain developed a system of public health which was to form the basis of the modern National Health Service.

Christian charity played a part in the growth of public health. Individuals such as Lord Shaftesbury and Dr Barnardo tried to improve the conditions of the poor. Some caring industrialists gave money to the local voluntary hospitals; it became socially desirable to be on the board of a local hospital.

Fear of mob violence also played a part in wringing improvements from the upper classes. Reforms were granted to avoid the revolutions that swept many of the countries of mainland Europe in 1789–1815, 1830 and 1848. Some people realised that poverty created brutish behaviour, not the other way around. 'A man who comes home to a poor, comfortless hovel after his day's labour ... is too apt to fly for a temporary refuge to the alehouse or beer-shop,' wrote the chairman of the Bedford Poor Law

SOURCE 3

'A Court for King Cholera'
A famous *Punch* cartoon suggesting that cholera was caused by unhygienic, over-crowded conditions.

Union in 1842. In this way, public health became also a religious and moral issue.

Another pressure was terror of disease. Cholera was the most feared (there were epidemics in 1831–32, 1848–49, 1854 and 1865–66). There were epidemics of typhoid fever in 1826–27, 1831–32, 1837 and 1846–47. Tuberculosis was endemic (permanently present); it accounted for about 20 per cent of all deaths. Although confined for the most part to poor areas, these diseases occasionally 'escaped' and killed rich people. 'One visible Blessing seems already to be coming upon us through the alarm of cholera. Every rich man is now obliged to look into the miserable bye-lanes and corners inhabited by the Poor; and many crying abuses are ... about to be remedied,' wrote Dorothy Wordsworth in 1831.

Most remarkably of all, the public health movement benefited from the desire to pay *less* for the poor, not more. The Poor Law Amendment Act of 1834 had abolished out-relief (payments of money to poor people). The poor were given help only if they went into a workhouse (this was to stop people claiming poor relief until they were absolutely desperate). Even so, the workhouses filled up with the sick, the aged and the infirm. Meanwhile, the Act had required every Poor Law district to appoint a medical officer. These men drew attention to 'the large amount of money which the public have had to pay in support of the sick, and the families of the sick'. At least one-fifth of all cases of poverty, they said, were caused by illness, and any spending on public health improvements to prevent disease 'would ultimately amount to less than the cost of the disease'. In this way they argued that investing in public health measures would *save* the ratepayers' money.

Conditions in the nineteenth century

SOURCE A

'Over London by Rail'
An engraving (1875) by Gustave Doré, a French artist. Doré produced hundreds of engravings of London – many of them while he was living in Paris.

SOURCE B

'Wentworth Street, Whitechapel'
An engraving (c. 1870) by Gustave Doré.

SOURCE C

Darlington Streets in 1851

January 1851
Bank Top... The streets here are neither paved nor drained & the numerous yards are so constructed as effectually to prevent all ventilation, and abound with filthy pigsty's and horrible privvies.

December 1851
On the night of the 19th... I visited an Irish family in Clayrow and assembled in a room of less than 10 feet square, I found 5 men 3 women and 3 children two of whom were covered with smallpox! There was no furniture except two broken chairs, two filthy beds lay rolled up upon the floor, and some dirty clothes hung drying from a cord which was stretched across the room. Near to the fireplace stood a pail full of the most detestable messes, whilst fronting the window was an open dunghill, & an uncovered drain exhaled its nauseous odours close to the door.

A family residing in Bondgate had been using the water from one of the rain butts for some weeks, and finding it exceedingly offensive, the vessel was examined, when the source of contamination was found to proceed from the decomposing body of a child which had been saturating there for more than a month!

J.E. Piper, *Darlington Local Board of Health, Officer of Health Report Book*, 1851. Piper had been appointed Officer of Health for Darlington by the Local Board of Health (see page 36).

SOURCE E

Lillie Langtry's bedroom, c. 1896
Miss Langtry, an actress, was considered one of the most beautiful women of her time. She became the mistress of the future Edward VII.

SOURCE F

Two nations

The approaches to the town of Darlington give the idea of wealth, cleanliness and comfort—so many handsome residences and tastefully laid out grounds... whilst the streets for the most part are lengthy and wide... From these streets ramify numerous dirty lanes, dark passages, narrow alleys and crowded courts and yards, undrained, badly paved, ill supplied with air, light and water, where disgusting nuisances [health hazards] abound.

J.E. Piper, *Darlington Local Board of Health, Officer of Health Report Book*, December 1851.

SOURCE D

Woodland Road, Darlington, in the late nineteenth century
Note that this is a middle-class area: a fire in every room, and the children are wearing shoes!

Questions

1 Identify 30 of the health hazards in Sources A–C.

2 Analyse your list of health hazards (i.e. divide your list up into different kinds of hazard). Compare the categories you have chosen with those of other pupils.

3 What impression do you get from the sources of the state of public health in the early nineteenth century?

4 List the health hazards you can see in Sources D and E. How many can you find?

5 Compare this list with your list of health hazards from Sources A–C. In what ways are the lists different? What different impression do they give of public health in the nineteenth century?

6 Read Source F. Use it to suggest one explanation of why Sources A–C are so different from Sources D and E. Examine all the sources carefully. Can you suggest any other possible reasons why the two sets of sources seem so different?

The Public Health Act

In 1842 Edwin Chadwick, one of the Poor Law commissioners, organised the production of a *Report on the Sanitary Condition of the Labouring Population of Great Britain*. This was a vast compendium of all the evils and bad conditions in Britain's towns. The investigators asked questions such as: 'When were you last washed?' ('When I was last in prison' was a frequent answer.) It summarised all the arguments for improved public health (**Source 4**).

Nevertheless, it was not until six years after the report, and under the pressure of another cholera epidemic, that the Public Health Act (1848) was passed. This Act created a central General Board of Health and allowed towns to set up local boards of health (if one-tenth of the ratepayers wanted one). The local boards could, if they wished, appoint a medical officer of health, clean streets and provide sewers. The board's engi-neer, John Roe, constructed small, egg-shaped sewers that could be easily flushed, rather than the large sewers that had previously been built.

It is hard to understand today how anybody could oppose the General Board of Health. Many did so. Only 183 towns (out of nearly 500 in England and Wales) set up local boards. Few of the boards that were set up appointed

SOURCE 4

The case for public health

Most claims to poor relief are on the ground of destitution occasioned by sickness …

The various forms of epidemic and endemic disease are caused chiefly amongst the labouring classes by atmospheric impurities produced by decomposing animal and vegetable substances, by damp and filth, and close and overcrowded dwellings … Where those circumstances are removed by drainage and by proper cleansing and better ventilation …, such disease almost entirely disappears …

The formation of all habits of cleanliness is obstructed by defective supplies of water.

The annual loss of life from filth and bad ventilation are greater than the loss from death or wounds in any wars in which the country has been engaged in modern times …

[Bad conditions] produce an adult population [which is] short-lived, improvident, reckless, and intemperate … The removal of unhealthy physical circumstances, and the promotion of town, household, and personal cleanliness, are necessary to the improvement of the moral condition of the population.

Report on the Sanitary Condition of the Labouring Population of Great Britain, 1842.
destitution: poverty
endemic: always present
improvident: wasteful
intemperate: drunken

DATAPOINT

Edwin Chadwick

SOURCE 5

Edwin Chadwick (1800–90)

- Born in Lancashire in 1800, Chadwick first trained as a barrister, supporting himself by writing.

- In 1828 he wrote an article on poverty in London in the Westminster Review. This led to him becoming the secretary of the famous reformer Jeremy Bentham.

- In February 1832, Chadwick was asked to be an assistant commissioner to the Royal Commission on the Poor Laws. In 1833 he became a full commissioner, and greatly influenced the Commission's recommenda-tions.

medical officers of health. The Act was only temporary and when its term expired in 1854 the three commissioners – Lord Shaftesbury, Chadwick and Southwood Smith – were forced to resign. The General Board of Health continued with reduced powers until 1858, when it was abolished.

- In 1834 he was appointed secretary to the new Poor Law Board. It was as secretary that he noticed how much poverty was caused by illness.

- Even Chadwick's friends recognised that he could be unpleasant and domineering, and he became very unpopular.

- In 1838 the commissioners persuaded him to devote his time to the public health issue. Using information gathered by the Poor Law medical officers, Chadwick produced the *Report on the Sanitary Condition of the Labouring Population of Great Britain* (1842).

- In 1844 he became a member of the Health of the Towns Association, which campaigned for improvements in public health.

- When the Royal Commission on Large Towns was appointed in 1844, although he was not on the commission, Chadwick attended its meetings, devised its questions, conducted the interviews and wrote the report!

- In 1848 he was appointed full-time paid commissioner of the Public Health Board, and energetically began to implement the Public Health Act. His methods and character, however, made him many enemies.

- When the Public Health Board came up for renewal in 1854, Chadwick was forced to resign. Parliament voted him a pension of £1000 a year in gratitude for his services to the nation, but he was not given another post.

Knowledge and understanding

Use Chapter 4 to answer these questions on the causes of the improvement in public health in the nineteenth century. The questions will also help you to analyse the importance of the individual within the process of historical change.

1 Suggest a number of reasons why the rich often failed to help the poor in nineteenth-century Britain.

2 Many historians believe that the Poor Law Amendment Act of 1834 was the beginning of the modern British welfare state. Suggest reasons why they believe this.

3 What did John Roe contribute to the health of the nineteenth-century British public?

4 What did Chadwick think was the cause of disease (Source 4)? What is the name for this theory of the cause of disease (see page 31)? Why did the British develop a public health system before they understood about germs?

5 Using pages 32–33, make your own notes on the different reasons why public health progressed in the first half of the nineteenth century.

6 Look again at the list of preconditions for change on page 30. How many of them had been fulfilled by 1848?

7 Read the **Datapoint** on Edwin Chadwick and the account of the public health movement on pages 32–37.
a Make a list of all the ways in which Chadwick helped to advance the cause of public health.
b In what ways did he hold it back?
c How important was Chadwick compared to the issues you identified in answer to Questions 4–6?

8 Write an essay:
How important was Edwin Chadwick in the development of public health in Britain in the nineteenth century?
Writing the assignment:
- You must measure Chadwick's contribution to public health against the other factors.
- Using a paragraph for each point,
  either
  deal with Chadwick's achievements in turn (Question 7), discussing for each how other factors were more / less important;
  or
  deal with the other factors in turn (Questions 4–6), discussing how Chadwick contributed to each one.
- Then write a final paragraph summing up Chadwick's importance.

The 'dirty party'

The problem with history is that the records are kept by the victors. Shaftesbury, Chadwick and their supporters labelled their opponents the 'dirty party'. Historians often quote the comment of *The Times* on 1 August 1854 that 'we prefer to take our chance of cholera and the rest, than to be bullied into health. There is nothing a man so hates ... as having his pet dunghill cleared away'. It makes the opponents of the Board of Health look stupid.

Were the 'dirty party' really so stupid? This investigation will let you consider both sides of the picture.

SOURCE B
Mr Chadwick's failings

Having stated what he regarded as Mr Chadwick's merits, he would not disguise that, like many other ardent reformers, Mr Chadwick very often, in his zeal for change, overlooked or disregarded the objections and repugnance with which his views were received by others ... It was very probable that Mr Chadwick had not observed towards these persons the most conciliatory tone.

Report of the speech by Lord John Russell in parliament, 31 July 1854.

SOURCE A
Our enemies

Our enemies include the civil engineers, because we have selected able men, who have carried into effect new principles, and at a less salary. The College of Physicians, because of our success at dealing with the cholera, when we proved that many a Poor Law medical officer knew more than all the flash and fashionable doctors of London. Then come the water companies, for we devised a method of supply, which altogether replaced them. The Commissioners of Sewers, for our plans and principles were the reverse of theirs; they hated us with a pure hatred.

Lord Shaftesbury's diary entry for 9 August 1853.

SOURCE C
Why oppose the Board of Health?

As to the necessity of a Public Health Board, no one denied it. . . The present Board, however, had been a misfortune and a mischief rather than an advantage to the country . . .

The Public Health Act permitted an interference with every trade and every occupation . . . Inspectors might enter any house they pleased, order what improvements they chose to call so, and take the cost from the owners . . .

The Act provided that if one-tenth of the ratepayers of a place should petition the Board of Health, [it should have to set up a local board of health]. This, of itself, was opposed to every principle of the Constitution, that one-tenth of the population was to govern all the rest.

He had great respect for Lord Shaftesbury's character, but he entirely objected to the noble Earl's grand principle of government – the centralisation of everything – the interfering with everything and everybody.

The noble Earl said that the cholera was approaching. The cholera was always coming whenever the powers of the Board of Health were about to expire. . . He did not wish to interfere with the Public Health Act, but he desired that it should be differently administered.

Report of the speech made by Lord Seymour in parliament against the renewal of the Board of Public Health, 31 July 1854.

Lord Seymour was the leader of the opposition to the Public Health Board.

SOURCE D

Not for nothing

The strong opposition against the Board had not arisen for nothing.

Report of part of the speech made by Mr Henley in parliament, 31 July 1854.

SOURCE E

What went wrong?

The records read like a Greek tragedy. Everything went wrong... [The Board began work] during the period of a cholera epidemic... Chadwick and his colleagues were grossly overworked. One inspector had cholera and another had fever. [Chadwick] commented, 'It may be said the Board of Health is very unwell.'

In 1853, there was a new cholera epidemic which started in Croydon soon after a local board of health had been set up, and new pipes installed. The suspicion arose that *the cholera was waterborne*... The miasma theory was utterly discredited, and so was the ill-fated General Board of Health.

Kathleen Jones, *The Making of Social Policy 1830–1990*, 1991.

SOURCE F

'Cholera Pie'

The 19th-century cartoonist Robert Cruikshank suggests that the doctors grew rich as a result of epidemics.

Questions

1 Read Source A. Make a list of all the people who opposed Shaftesbury.

2 What, according to Shaftesbury, were the motives of his opponents? Does he admit that any of them have a valid reason for opposing him? Suggest reasons why he presents them in this way.

3 Using Sources B–F, list all the reasons given by Shaftesbury's opponents for their opposition. Were they really the 'dirty party'?

4 Write the playscript of a discussion between two people. One person supports Shaftesbury, the other supports Lord Seymour. They are discussing the rights and wrongs of the debate over public health, 1848–54. Both are aware of all the sources and information in this chapter.

Writing the assignment:
- Speaker 1 will tell Speaker 2 what some person on his or her side said. He or she will explain how this demonstrates the truth of his or her side of the argument.
- Speaker 2 will reply first of all by explaining how that statement is unreliable (biased, not true, etc.) Then he or she will tell Speaker 1 what some person on his or her side said.
- So the discussion will proceed until every issue has been dealt with. There is no need for either side to win.

The Progress of Public Health card game

The pictures on pages 40–41 represent the main events in the development of public health in Britain from 1830 to 1875. You may find it helpful to photocopy the pages. You could then cut the pictures into cards, which you can lay out on the table and arrange and rearrange as necessary.

Analysis

1 Take out of the sequence all those cards which are specifically Acts of Parliament aimed to improve public health. Analyse them, i.e. divide them into piles, each one representing a different public health issue.
2 Find three examples of 'enabling' Acts (which gave permission for local authorities to act if they wished, but did not compel them to act). Find three Acts which compelled authorities to act.
3 Look carefully at the terms of the 1875 Public Health Act. It was a 'consolidating' Act. Work out what this means.

Causation

4 Find four cards which prove that the government knew there was a problem.
5 Find a card showing an event which you think may have stimulated the government to act. Find a card showing an event which was the result of that stimulus. Find two other such 'cause-consequence' linked cards.

Progress and change

6 Pick out a sequence of four cards which shows something developing through time. Explain your choice.
7 Select a series of cards to explain the idea: 'Today we would find the pace of change during the early years of the Industrial Revolution impossibly slow.'
8 Identify an event or sequence of events which you think was the turning point in the history of public health. Explain your choice.
9 Progress in history is rarely smooth. Find an example of a time when the cause of public health had a setback.
10 Progress in history is often unplanned and haphazard. Find an example of an Act of Parliament which proved to be inadequate and had to be improved later.

Use the ideas you have developed while playing the card game to:
Write an account of the developments which led to the Public Health Act of 1875.

1831–32
Cholera epidemic.

1840
Public vaccination against smallpox is provided free for children.

1831–32
Temporary central and local boards of health are set up, but abolished after the epidemic.

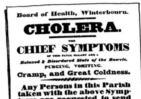

1842
Report on the Sanitary Condition of the Labouring Population of Great Britain.

1832
Dr J. P. Kay's book describes the terrible *Moral and Physical Conditions of the Working Classes.*

1845
Report of the Commission on Large Towns.

1834
The Poor Law Amendment Act appoints Poor Law medical officers.

1846
An Act to encourage Public Baths and Wash-houses is introduced.

1836
An Act for the Registration of Births, Marriages and Deaths is introduced.

1848
Public Health Act
A central General Board of Health is created, and local boards of health may be set up which can: appoint a medical officer of health; provide sewers; pave and clean streets; inspect meat; inspect lodging houses; control burial grounds.

1848–49
Cholera epidemic.

1858
The General Board of Health is abolished.

1871
The Vaccination Acts Amendment enforces the 1853 Act.

1853
Vaccination is made compulsory, although the Act does not establish any powers to compel its enforcement.

1865–66
Cholera epidemic.

1874
The Registration Act requires doctors to sign death certificates stating the cause of death.

1854
Chadwick is dismissed. The General Board of Health loses most of its power.

1866
A Sanitary Act compels local authorities to take action on sewerage, water and street cleaning, and also smoke, overcrowding and infection.

1875
The Artisans Dwellings Act: owners of houses are responsible for their upkeep and repair. Local authorities may buy and demolish slum areas.

1854
Cholera epidemic.

1867
The Parliamentary Reform Act greatly increases the number of people who can vote.

BALLOT BOX

1875
Public Health Act
This Act organises existing legislation on public health under 11 headings: sewerage and drainage, privvies, cleansing, water supply, lodging houses, nuisances, offensive trades, unsound meat, infectious diseases and hospitals, prevention of epidemic diseases, and mortuaries.

1855
The Nuisance Removal Act makes overcrowded housing illegal.

1868
The Torrens Act encourages the improvement of property and the demolition of slum buildings.

5 Steady Advance?

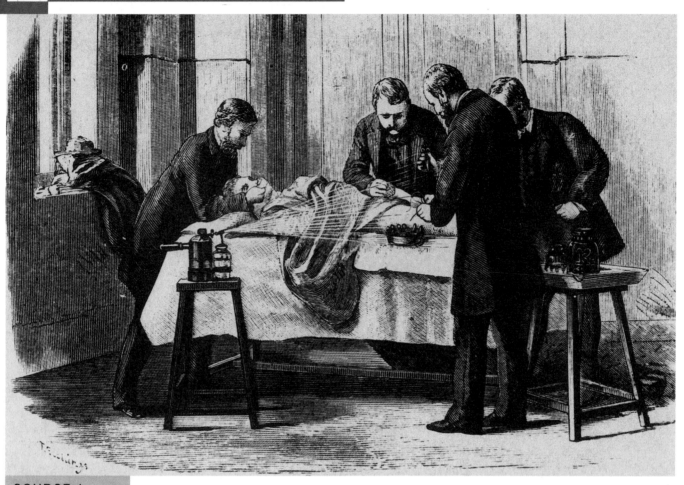

SOURCE 1

An operation in the 1870s
For the first time it was possible to go into hospital for an operation, expecting to recover. Note Lister's antiseptic spray, and the anaesthetist.

Most of the changes that shape our lives – for instance, leaving home or choosing a career – do not happen suddenly, out of the blue. They have usually been developing slowly and quietly over a long period of time, often without anyone noticing (even, sometimes, ourselves). On the surface, the century before 1946 seems to be merely 'the years before the welfare state'. But was it during these years that the foundations of the modern welfare state were laid?

The late nineteenth and early twentieth centuries were a time of rapid medical advance. The greatest improvements occurred in the hospitals, notably the use of anaesthetics to prevent pain, and the introduction of antiseptics, which killed germs (see the Datapoints on pages 43 and 44).

SOURCE 2

A doctor at work in 1892

I had my tonsils out when I was 19 ... I stood up opposite [the doctor] and he showed me the instrument he was going to use and I handled it and saw how it worked. There was no anaesthetic, no hospital, no nurse. I opened my mouth wide ... the cutting edge of the instrument ... was fitted over one tonsil, and the doctor pushed the cutter through the tonsil and cut it off. It was certainly a painful and trying ordeal, and I was given a few minutes to recover, and then the same process was repeated at the other side. After a short while, to attend the bleeding, I walked home (about a mile).

Letter from Mr C.R.H. Pickard to *The Guardian*, 15 February 1968.
This passage contains the memories of a 95-year-old man.

Florence Nightingale and nursing

Many books about Florence Nightingale concentrate on her struggle with her parents to be allowed to become a nurse, and on her success in the British army hospital (in Scutari, Turkey) during the Crimean War, where she reduced the death rate from 42 per cent to 2 per cent.

Her greatest contribution to the improvement of medicine, however, occurred in the years after she returned to Britain in 1856. Although bedridden, using her fame as 'the lady with the lamp' she:

* published *Notes on Nursing* (1859). It became a best seller and was translated into French, German and Italian;
* founded the Nightingale School for Nurses (1860); 1452 nurses had trained there by 1897, although only 864 had completed the year's training and gained jobs in hospitals.

Florence Nightingale required her nurses to be 'Sober, Honest, Truthful, Trustworthy, Punctual, Quiet and Orderly, Cleanly and Neat'. They were trained:

> '... in the dressing of blisters, burns, sores, wounds, and in applying poultices and minor dressings. In the application of leeches, externally and internally. In the management of helpless Patients, i.e. moving, changing, personal cleanliness of feeding, keeping warm (or cool), preventing and dressing bed sores ... In making the beds of the Patients, and removal of sheets whilst Patient is in bed. To be competent to cook gruel, arrowroot, egg-flip, puddings, drinks for the sick. To understand ventilation ... To make strict observations of the sick ...'

In the early nineteenth century many nurses had been people of low repute, thieves and drunkards. Florence Nightingale is generally regarded as the founder of nursing as a profession.

SOURCE 3

Florence Nightingale (1820–1910).

SOURCE 4

'The Victorian Doctor'
A painting by the Victorian artist Sir Luke Fildes. What elements of despair can you see in the scene?

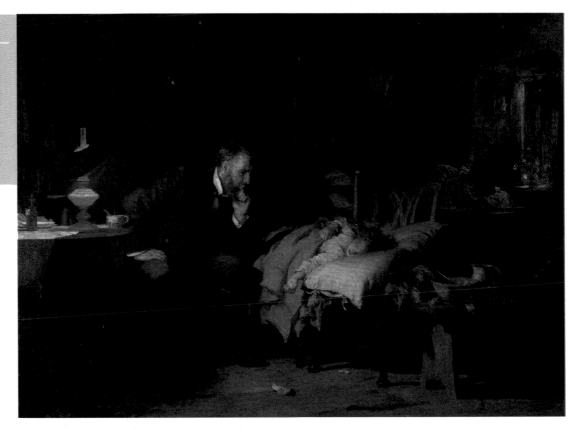

D A T A P O I N T

Key medical advances of the nineteenth century

1845 The American dentist Horace Wells uses laughing gas as an anaesthetic.

1846 The American surgeon Dr John C. Warren uses ether as an anaesthetic for an amputation.

1847 The Scottish doctor James Simpson discovers that chloroform can be used as an anaesthetic.

1855 John Snow, author of *The Mode of Communication of Cholera*, proves that cholera is a waterborne disease.

1864 The French scientist Louis Pasteur proves that bacteria (germs) cause disease.

1865 The Scottish surgeon Robert Lister develops antiseptic surgery (killing the germs using carbolic acid spray).

1872 The German researcher Robert Koch discovers how to identify which germ causes which disease, and identifies the anthrax bacteria. He also discovers the germs which cause blood poisoning (1878) and tuberculosis (1882). Other scientists identify the germs which cause:
  - 1882 typhoid;
  - 1883 cholera;
  - 1884 tetanus;
  - 1886 pneumonia;
  - 1894 bubonic plague.

1880 One of Pasteur's researchers, Charles Chamberland, discovers that injecting weakened germs inoculates the body against a disease (the body learns how to defeat those germs). Scientists develop:
  - 1885 rabies inoculation;
  - 1890 a serum to prevent diptheria;
  - 1906 BCG vaccine against tuberculosis.

1890 The American surgeon W.S. Halsted uses rubber gloves during operations. The German doctor Herman Kimmel has already introduced the idea of 'scrubbing up'. It is the beginning of the idea of aseptic surgery (preventing any germs in the operating theatre).

1895 The German scientist Wilhelm K. von Röntgen discovers X-rays.

1890s The German scientist Paul Ehrlich develops the idea of antibodies ('magic bullets'). Some chemical substances are found which attack and kill germs:
  - 1891 methylene blue against malaria;
  - 1904 trypan red against sleeping sickness;
  - 1909 Salvarsan 606 against syphilis (VD).

SOURCE 5

Louis Pasteur at work
Compare this with the picture of the alchemist's laboratory (page 27). What progress has been made?

Knowledge and understanding

These questions will help you to investigate the paradox that the medical advances in the late nineteenth century did not lead to significant improvements in health. (You will find it interesting to compare your answers to these questions with your answers to the questions on page 26.)

1 Read the **Datapoint: Key medical advances of the nineteenth century** on this page. What impression does it give of health care in the late nineteenth century?

2 Look at Sources 2 and 4. What impression do they give of health care in the late nineteenth century?

3 Using the ideas you have gained answering Questions 1 and 2, explain the meaning of the following passage:
> 'From the point of view of a [doctor], increased knowledge … is naturally regarded as important professional advance. But from the point of view of the patient, none of these changes has any practical significance until such time as it contributes to the preservation of health or recovery from illness.'

T. McKeown, *The Modern Rise of Population*, 1976.

4 Suggest possible reasons why the great advances in medical knowlege at the end of the nineteenth century did not generally lead to improvements in the health of ordinary people.

5 Using pages 40–41 (the card game), make a list of the changes that had contributed to the improvement of the health of ordinary people by 1900. How are they different from the changes listed in the **Datapoint: Key medical advances of the nineteenth century**?

The failure of prevention

| In the late nineteenth century doctors were still largely unable to cure disease; curative medicine played only a minor part in the improving health of the nation.

The public health reforms of 1830–1875 had followed 'the preventative principle'. They aimed, by improving housing, water supplies and sanitation, to stop disease occurring. The public's health did, in fact, improve. The death rate fell from 22 to 17 per thousand over the period 1850–1901; in 1901 average life expectancy had reached 45.5 years (males) and 49 years (females).

Observers, however, noticed that the infant death rate remained high, at about 150 per thousand, and in 1899 it peaked at 163 per thousand. Charles Booth's *Life and Labour of the People in London* (1891–1903) described the poverty in which most people lived. A study of York by Benjamin Seebohm Rowntree (1897–98) revealed that 28 per cent of the population fell below the accepted minimum income, and 16 per cent lived in absolute poverty. It was clear that the Housing Acts were utterly failing to remove the slums in which people lived. 'It is a wonder that they are not found dead in their wretched dens,' wrote one journalist in a series of articles called *Horrible London*.

A few private individuals tried to improve housing. The American millionaire George Peabody (1795–1869) created the Peabody Trust, which built and rented good quality housing in Britain and America. Model villages were built by wealthy industrialists such as Lord Leverhulme (Port Sunlight, 1888) and George and Richard Cadbury (Bourneville, 1895). In 1899 Ebenezer Howard formed the Garden City Association, which began campaigning for planned towns with open spaces, tree-lined streets and houses with gardens. The first garden city, Letchworth, was founded in 1903 (soon followed by Hampstead and Welwyn). It gradually became clear, however, that the state needed to do something about housing.

The breakthrough

| During the Boer War in South Africa (1899–1902) the government became alarmed when it found out that almost half the volunteers for the army were medically unfit to serve. As one writer to the *Morning Post* in 1900 commented: 'Lack of good food, good clothes and good air in children is the main reason why some 50 per cent of our urban working-class population is unfit to bear arms.'

The Liberal politician Lloyd George complained bitterly that Britain had spent £250 million on a war to avenge an insult by Boer farmers in South Africa, but was 'not ashamed to see her children walking the streets hungry and in rags'. He commented in 1910: 'I hope our competition with Germany will not be in armaments alone.' (Britain's military rival, Germany, was known to have an excellent system of social welfare.)

The Liberal government (1905–11), therefore, passed a string of Acts of Parliament which followed what historians call 'the personal principle' – they were state measures designed to improve the health of the individual citizen. These are listed in detail in the **Datapoint: Public health 1875–1914** on page 46.

Most important of all was the National Health Insurance Act (1911). One writer of the time called it 'the greatest scheme of social reconstruction ever yet attempted'. It created the doctor's panel (list of patients), the insurance stamp, sickness benefit and the local GP – all of which have survived to the present day. Workers who fell ill were paid ten shillings a week, and the GPs were paid nine shillings a year for each patient on their panel.

DATAPOINT

Public health 1875–1914

1889 *Act for the Prevention of Cruelty to Children*

1890 *Housing of the Working Classes Act*
Town councils are allowed to buy land to clear slums; building standards for new housing are laid down.

1902 *Midwives Act*
Makes training of midwives compulsory.

1906 *Education (Provision of Meals) Act*
An enabling Act which allows local authorities to provide free school meals to poor pupils. Infant Welfare Centres are set up.

1907 *Education (Administrative Provisions) Act*
The School Medical Service is created. It is said by some historians to be 'the first personal health service established by Act of Parliament'.

1907 *Notification of Births Act*
Health Visitors are appointed to call on families.

1908 *Children's Act* (the 'Children's Charter')
Negligence becomes a crime; children are forbidden to beg or smoke.

1909 *Old Age Pensions*
Every person over 70 receives five shillings (25p) a week. In 1914 five shillings could buy: two pounds of meat, four loaves of bread, half a pound of butter, five pints of milk and ten eggs.

1909 *Housing and Town Planning Act*
Back-to-back housing is prohibited. All local authorities have to appoint a Medical Officer of Health.

1909 *The People's Budget*
To pay for improved social services, David Lloyd George, the Prime Minister, increases income tax, imposes a land tax on landowners, and introduces supertax on incomes over £3000 per annum.

1911 *National Health Insurance Act*
Introduces compulsory health insurance for all workers who earn less than £160 a year. The employee contributes fourpence (about 2p) a week, the employer threepence and the state twopence. The workers are put on a doctor's panel and receive free medical treatment. Their families, however, still have to pay for their treatment.

SOURCE 6

This *Punch* cartoon of 22 November 1911 suggests that everybody was unhappy about Lloyd George's reforms – not only the rich man and woman in the middle of the boat, but even the maid and the working man in the back!

THE PITILESS PHILANTHROPIST.

MR. LLOYD GEORGE. "NOW UNDERSTAND, I'VE BROUGHT YOU OUT TO DO YOU GOOD, AND *GOOD I WILL DO YOU*, WHETHER YOU LIKE IT OR NOT."

Investigation

The dawn of hope?

THE DAWN OF HOPE.

NATIONAL INSURANCE
AGAINST SICKNESS
AND DISABLEMENT

Mr. LLOYD GEORGE'S National Health Insurance Bill provides for the insurance of the Worker in case of Sickness.

Support the Liberal Government
in their policy of
SOCIAL REFORM.

SOURCE A
Liberal Party poster, 1911.

SOURCE C
A confidence trick

It is a curiosity of twentieth-century history that this Act . . . is regarded as a piece of Socialist legislation, the first step in a vast social revolution. Yet the whole purpose of the National Insurance Act was anti-Socialist . . . to take the sting out of Socialist agitation . . .

The National Insurance Act was a confidence trick . . . Lloyd George publicised health insurance as a matter of the worker getting 'ninepence for fourpence'. The truth was that the worker paid for his benefits not only through his fourpence a week but also through general taxation. In effect, healthy and employed workers were being forced to subsidise sick and unemployed workers.

L.C.B. Seaman, *Post-Victorian Britain*, 1966. Seaman was a retired teacher. He believed that the most important event of the twentieth century was the rise of the Labour Party, and that the Liberal Party fell from importance because it failed to support change.

SOURCE B
The grand achievement

It was Lloyd George who launched the Liberal and Radical forces of this country effectively into the broad stream of social betterment and social security . . . He was the champion of the weak and the poor . . . Most people are unconscious of how much their lives have been shaped by the laws for which Lloyd George was responsible . . . I was his lieutenant in those bygone days, and shared in a minor way in the work.

Winston Churchill, speaking in the House of Commons, 28 March 1945. Churchill was announcing the death of Lloyd George. In 1911 Churchill had been a Liberal MP, President of the Board of Trade, and an ally of Lloyd George. (A Radical is someone who wants major social and political changes – in this sense, a socialist politician.)

Questions

The election poster
1 Compare Source A with Source 4 (on page 43). What was the message of the poster?

2 Why is the message of the poster so positive? Can it be trusted as a source by a historian who wants to evaluate the National Insurance Act? Explain your answer.

The obituary
3 List the positive things Churchill says about Lloyd George.

4 What motives can you find in Source B for Churchill to present an over-rosy view of Lloyd George?

The historian
5 Use the **Datapoint: Public health 1875–1914** to explain the slogan 'ninepence for fourpence'.

6 List the negative things that Seaman says about the National Insurance Act.

7 Explain why, given his view of history, Seaman might have been tempted to be critical about Lloyd George's actions.

Analysis
8 Discuss which of the authors in Sources A–C is most likely to have taken an objective, considered view.

9 Make a list of rules for historians who want to be fair when they are studying the past.

10 Write an essay:
Was Lloyd George's National Insurance Act of 1911 a triumph or a trick?
Writing the assignment:
Write the essay in three sections: firstly, the opinion you least agree with; secondly, the opinion you most agree with; then your own ideas. For each, cite the evidence which supports that opinion, but then explain how that evidence is of doubtful reliability. For your own ideas, explain how these overcome the difficulties presented by the evidence and are as objective as possible.

The silent revolution

During the First World War (1914–18) more than 8.5 million military personnel had died; the 'Spanish flu' of 1918 killed 25 million people worldwide in a single year. It was a timely reminder to the government that humankind had greater enemies than the Germans. There was also a feeling in Britain of the need to create 'a land fit for the heroes' who had fought in the war.

After the war, therefore, the government continued to enact personal hygiene measures. Tuberculosis sanatoria and the first large-scale programmes to build council houses all come from this period. The local government reorganisation of 1929 put hundreds of Poor Law hospitals under the control of the local authorities. The government started to give free milk to school children and many local authorities provided free school dinners (and sometimes breakfasts and teas) for poor children. These were the 'cod-liver oil years', when men such as Sir Edward Mellanby (see page 60) tried to make people aware of the need for the proper balance of vitamins in children's food and recommended that they should have a daily dose of cod-liver oil. Trips to the seaside, swimming, rambling, climbing and youth hostelling all became popular during this period.

At the same time there was rapid medical advance. Scientists developed new drugs such as Prontosil (a sulphonamide, made from chemicals derived from coal tar) and penicillin (an antibiotic, derived from living materials such as fungi). Now doctors could actually cure infectious diseases and post-operative blood poisoning. Blood transfusions became common after the development of the continual drip method by Harnott and Kekwick in 1935.

By the end of the interwar period, all local authorities employed health visitors, sanitary inspectors and a medical officer of health. They cleared slums, disposed of sewage, collected refuse, inspected food and controlled pests. They ran vaccination programmes, maternity and health clinics, swimming baths, parks, and water, gas and electricity services. In 1929 the city of Leeds claimed that 'Leeds Corporation … nurses and shields inhabitants from the cradle to the grave'.

By 1931 average life expectancy had increased to 58.4 (males) and 62.4 years of age (females). Some historians believe that during the interwar years there was a 'silent revolution' which changed people's attitudes and created the political will to try to deal with poverty and disease.

SOURCE 7

A family living in Woking, Surrey, in 1921
Their home is, literally, a pigsty.

Knowledge and understanding

Use pages 45–51 to answer the following questions.

1 What is the difference between 'preventative' and 'personal' public health measures?

2 List the health services offered by local authorities by the end of the 1930s.

3 Looking back on the 1930s, one Labour politician called them 'a period of steady and purposeful social advance'. Do you agree?

SOURCE 8

Alexander Fleming, the discoverer of penicillin, the first antibiotic medicine, in 1928. Compare this picture with the pictures of Pasteur (page 44) and the 17th century alchemist (page 27) at work. What changes do you see?

D A T A P O I N T

Public health 1918–1939

1919 *Ministry of Health Act*
The ministry is set up. It administers the prevention and cure of disease; the mentally and physically disabled; the blind; research; the training of doctors, dentists, midwives, health visitors and sanitary inspectors. Its medical departments are organised into ten sections, including: epidemiology (the study of diseases); maternity and child welfare; tuberculosis; food; sanitation; research laboratories; and school medical services.

1919 *Housing and Planning Act*
Local authorities are required to provide proper housing; government grants are provided.

1919 *Nurses Registration Act*
Sets up a state register of qualified nurses; to qualify, nurses have to complete three years' training and pass two examinations.

1920 *Dawson Report*
Recommends the setting up of health centres.

1921 *Tuberculosis Act*
Local authorities are required to set up sanatoria for tuberculosis patients.

1924 *Wheatley Housing Act*
Sets a 15-year plan for building council houses (half a million built by 1933); local authorities are allowed to subsidise rents from the rates.

1929 *Local Government Act*
The old Poor Law Unions are abolished. Many workhouses become public hospitals for the aged and chronically ill.

1934 *Free School Milk Act*
Gives a third of a pint of milk to each pupil every day (not compulsory).

1934 *Unemployment Assistance Board*
This takes over control of payments to the unemployed – 24 shillings a week for a married couple (£1.20) – provided they take the hated 'means test' to prove they do not have any money. The UAB also provides a number of other social welfare services, including advice on matters of health and housing.

1936 *Public Health Act*
A consolidating Act. Hospitals must provide out-patient departments.

How good were 'the good old days'?

SOURCE A

Marion Clare remembers

My father was 'on the panel' – and we paid one shilling a week, or something like that, and then we were all covered and the doctor used to come to our house. We were quite hard up, but we were never without medical treatment. We were on Dr Metcalfe's panel. If you were registered sick and on the panel you had to be in by 9 o'clock; you weren't allowed to go out in the evening.

I remember the doctor coming when we had measles and chickenpox. They didn't just come once. They would look in every day whilst you were ill, and then every few days when you were on the mend. There was a different attitude. The doctors in those days were always so lovely, so nice. They were a friend of the family. They'd probably brought you into the world, and they knew your parents and your grandparents.

They had all kinds of services for children, too. When one of our neighbours had her baby she stopped eating to feed her husband, because they hadn't enough for both of them when he was unemployed. The baby started having convulsions. The health visitor used to go round a lot; she made her go to the local clinic every lunchtime, and they gave her a meal there, so that her milk would be rich enough to feed the baby. Dentists and eye-doctors came to the school. A nurse came to look for nits. They go on about the National Health Service being so fantastic, but really it seems to me that we were a lot better off under the panel system.

As a teenager I was poorly a lot. They hadn't a clue what was the matter with me; they just used to say it was 'debility'. It was only when I was an adult that they discovered the scar on my lung left by TB. I must have had a very mild bout of TB, because I recovered on my own. Everybody was frightened of tuberculosis in those days – much more than cancer nowadays – many people died of it. They used to have sanatoria, and people would go away for six or nine months. They'd be totally isolated. They'd leave the doors open all the time, winter and summer, to let the fresh air in. When your father was young he had scarlet fever, and they put him in an isolation hospital for six weeks. His parents were only allowed to look at him through a glass window.

Family Medicine

In those days you didn't go to the doctor first. Your mother had all kinds of remedies handed down through the family. We used to have cod-liver oil and malt. And brimstone and treacle! My mother would mix up this yellow brimstone in a saucer with some treacle. We used to hate taking it; it gave you the most awful wind and diarrhoea. If you had an upset tummy you would take a patent medicine called Composition 'to warm your stomach' – it probably had ginger in it. If you were off your food you'd have Parish's Chemical Food, or Dr Thompson's Slippery Elm Food – that's great stuff; we still have some in the cupboard. And Vick – they were great ones for rubbing things on you in those days, such as wintergreen

ointment for rheumatism. You had a gut feeling of what was needed for what, and then if that didn't work you'd go to the chemist and tell him, and he'd give you something to try. When I was a child I got warts on my hand. Every day after school I had to go to see Mr Taylor, the chemist, and he dabbed this stuff on my warts. He wouldn't give it to my mother. I suppose it was poison. Anyway, it cured my warts. You only went to the doctor if all else failed.

At the doctor's surgery

You queued in a long corridor, with chairs lined up down both sides. There were no appointments; you'd just go and sit and he would see you one at a time. It was an evening surgery; in those days the doctor went out on house calls all day. Surgery started at 6 o'clock and went on until he'd seen everybody. They were well thought of; people really trusted them.

His surgery had brown oil-cloth on the floor and a little, old-fashioned, popping gas fire (there was no fire at all in the corridor; you had to go wrapped up). There was a roll-top desk that was pushed back, with his prescription pad and stethoscope on it. He had a swivel chair, and there were a couple of chairs for the patients. It was a small, narrow room. They nearly always had the surgery in their own homes, and lived on the premises. He had an examination couch – it was covered with leather and was as hard as bone; I think it must have been packed with horsehair. But usually you stood to be examined. He had a stand with a lamp on top of it so he could shine it on you.

They'd mostly stopped doing operations in the surgery. However, when your father blew his hands up playing with chemicals when he was about nine years old, his sister took him on the bus to the surgery. He'd burst the artery, and he was bleeding badly, and the doctor sewed him up there in the surgery – without any anaesthetic! Nowadays they'd have rushed him off to hospital. The doctor was furious with him because he'd got blood all over his leather-topped table.

Hospitals

I think it was free to go into hospital, too. When I was three I went to the Eye and Ear Hospital to have my tonsils out, and they put me in a bed with another child, sleeping top to tail. They must have had some funny ideas about infection. I came round from the anaesthetic before the surgeon had finished. All I can remember is this huge black bushy beard, and an orange apron covered with blood, and this man shouting and getting angry. At the time I was terrified, because I thought he was shouting at me; it's only now that I realise he was shouting at the anaesthetist.

Interview with Marion Clare, 22 April 1993.
Marion Clare is the author's mother. She was born in 1924. Her father was a garage owner whose small business failed in the 1930s. She had to leave school at the age of 14, and took a job as a secretary. During the war she worked as a nurse. She married a chartered accountant and has been comfortably well-off ever since. She votes Conservative.

SOURCE C

Rapid progress?

There is little doubt that health standards rose rapidly between the wars. Millions of young men were medically examined for service in the armed forces between 1917 and 1918. Only 36 per cent were found to be perfectly fit and healthy whilst 41 per cent were either totally unfit or suffering from some serious disability. In 1939–45, using the same standards ... 70 per cent were put into the top grade and only 16 per cent in the two bottom grades. The same improvement applied to children. Ten-year-old children in one large city [Leeds] were found to be about 3 inches [7.62 cm] taller and 9 pounds [4 kg] heavier in 1938 than children of the same age in 1920. The number of children who died during their first year fell by one-third between 1921–35, as did the number of tuberculosis deaths during the same period ...

Medical services were also considerably improved. The National Health Insurance Act of 1911 covered 15 million persons by 1921 and 20 million by 1938 ... More than 3,500 welfare clinics for infants and nearly 1,800 ante-natal clinics were opened between 1918 and 1938.

J. Salt and B.J. Elliot, *British Society 1870–1970*, 1975. Salt and Elliot are social historians taking an overview of the period as a whole.

SOURCE B

A scene from the BBC TV series *The Citadel*, starring Ben Cross
Compare this reconstruction of a doctor's surgery with Marion Clare's description in Source A.

SOURCE D

'Haves' and 'have-nots'

In 1924, Britain still continued to become more and more sharply divided between the 'haves' and the 'have-nots' ... For the children of the three million unemployed, and other desperately poor families, having to share a glass of milk was a part of everyday life between the wars ...

In the early 1920s the maximum an unemployed man with a wife and three children could receive was 29s. 3d. (about £1·48) a week. At the same period the British Medical Association estimated that a family of this size needed to spend at least 22s. 6d. (£1·13) on food every week to remain in reasonable health ...

One of the worst aspects of life for these poor families was usually their appalling housing ... Many of them had only one tap, situated outside in the yard, to be shared by four or five families, and sometimes only one toilet, also outside in the yard.

The worst horror of these houses, though, were the bedbugs ... The great majority of slum-dwellers also suffered from head-lice ... Another grave problem between the Wars was that poor children were often inadequately fed ...

Not surprisingly, the slum children were constantly ill. Measles, diptheria and scarlet fever alone killed many thousands of poor children every year. The most dreaded disease was tuberculosis, though, which was often directly attributable to the children's poor living conditions and their inadequate diet.

F. Wilkins, *Growing Up Between the Wars*, 1979.

Questions

1 Make a list of the information that a historian can gain from Marion Clare's description of public health in Source A. Divide the list into 'facts' and 'opinions'.

2 Comparing the information about the health services in this section with your own experience of the present-day National Health Service, do you agree with Marion Clare that 'we were a lot better off under the panel system'? Suggest reasons why she said this.

3 Compare Source A with Sources C and D.
   a Suggest reasons why Source A might contain inaccuracies.
   b Use Sources C and D to comment on how reliable Source A seems to be.
   c In what ways does the information given in Source A differ from the information given in Source C? Explain your answer.

4 Complete the following with more than one idea:
   a Source A would be of little use to historians who wanted to ...
   b Source A would be of special use to historians who wanted to ...

5 Interview an old person who was alive during the 1930s, or listen to a recording of an old person's memories, or use Source A.
   Imagine you are a historical adviser for a television company that is producing a programme on *Health in the Thirties*. You have been sent an interview / recording / transcript of one old person's memories. Should the company use this in its programme?
   Write an evaluation for the director, advising him on how useful, representative and reliable the account is.
   Write your evaluation under three headings: *Strengths*, *Weaknesses* and *Recommendation*.

6 Towards Utopia?

Illness threatened the war effort. Would it not also damage production after the war?

Like King Midas' request that everything he touched might turn to gold, the National Health Service has not turned out to be quite the Utopia (perfect world) its originators thought it would be. Or has it?

Out of the inferno

In 1968 the historian Maurice Bruce suggested that 'the decisive event in the evolution of the Welfare State was the Second World War'.

When war broke out in 1939, the government evacuated large numbers of children from the cities to safer homes in the countryside. The middle-class families who looked after the evacuees were horrified at their poverty and ill-health. Many of the children were infested with lice and fleas. They had never worn underclothes, eaten food from a table, or slept in a bed. After initial anger at the parents, people realised that poverty, not neglect, was to blame.

The war also created a sense of togetherness which made middle-class people prepared to accept (and pay for) social reforms. In addition there was the realisation that, for poor people, rationing made them healthier and better fed than ever before, because it shared the resources of society more fairly. If the country could mobilise for warfare, it was said, why not for welfare? The government itself promoted this idea. In the later stages of the war, when Britain was winning, the Ministry of Information held out the hope of social reform to persuade people to keep up the war effort; it told people that they were fighting for a 'better Britain'.

The Beveridge Report

> Meanwhile, during the war, Britain was governed by a coalition National Government of politicians from all parties. As a result, Labour politicians found themselves in positions of power; Arthur Greenwood (a former Minister of Health) and Ernest Bevin (Minister of Labour and National Service) were both Labour politicians.

In June 1941, Greenwood asked Sir William Beveridge to chair a committee to look into the social services. Beveridge was an economist and civil servant who had long campaigned for social reform. His report, *Social Insurance and Allied Services*, was published in 1942. It was 300 pages long. According to *The Times*, it was as good a read as *Gone with the Wind* – it covered life 'from the cradle to the grave' and could not be finished in a single evening. Like *Gone with the Wind*, it became a best seller. People queued to buy it. Discussion groups were held in factories and offices to debate its recommendations. The Army Bureau of Current Affairs held classes to inform servicemen what it said.

The report declared that 'the object of government in peace and in war is not the glory of rulers or of races but the happiness of the common man'. As Beveridge summed it up in March 1943, its message was: 'Bread for everyone before cake for anybody.'

Beveridge wanted to destroy what he called the 'five giants on the road to reconstruction' – want, disease, ignorance, squalor, idleness. The answer, he said, was social security, a health service, free education, council housing and full employment. The result was a series of Acts of Parliament which set up the welfare state in Britain (see **Datapoint: The welfare state** on page 55). At the time it seemed as though there had been a revolution. One Labour politician called it 'D-Day in the battle for the new Britain'.

The struggle for the Health Service

> In the general election after the war (1945), Labour was elected into power. In 1946, Aneurin ('Ny') Bevan, Minister of Health, introduced the National Health Service Bill. It met with a great deal of opposition. There were some who feared the consequences of giving people free health care.

SOURCE 3

Aneurin Bevan
(1897–1960)

Many doctors opposed the National Health Service Bill. The government wanted to pay them a basic salary (instead of paying them according to the number of their patients). It also wanted to group them into health centres and place more GPs in the poorer areas of the country. It planned to bring all the voluntary hospitals under state control. Most doctors agreed 'that the present medical services of this country need to be developed and improved', but they feared a government dictatorship which would reduce them to civil servants, interfere in their work and harm their relationship with their patients.

Bevan, on the other hand, genuinely believed that 'medical treatment ... should be made available to rich and poor alike according to medical need and no other criteria'. He thought it wrong that hospitals should have to rely on gift days for their funding. But he had an abrasive personality. He did not believe that an elected minister should have to negotiate with those groups he called 'vested interests', such as the British Medical Association. There was a violent debate. Matters were not helped when Bevan described Conservative politicians as 'lower than vermin'.

Bevan gave way gradually. He reduced the basic salary to almost nothing, and continued to pay the doctors according to the number of patients on their panel. He allowed both doctors and consultants to take private paying clients as well as National Health patients. He promised not to interfere with doctors' medical decisions. By the 'appointed day' when the National Health Service came into being (see page 58) 18,500 of the 20,000 doctors had entered the service, and eight million additional people had applied to go on the doctors' panel lists, making a total of 30 million patients in all.

For the first time in history, Britain had a national, free, comprehensive medical service.

Knowledge and understanding

These questions will help you to consider Aneurin Bevan's role in the creation of the National Health Service. (You will find it interesting to compare your answers to these questions with your answers to the questions on page 37.)

1 Using pages 52–53, make your own notes on the different reasons why public health progressed in the years leading up to the NHS.

2 Look again at the list of 'preconditions for change' on page 30. How many of them were fulfilled by 1946?

3 From the text, make your own Datapoint on Aneurin Bevan.

4 In *The Creation of the NHS* (1967), A.J. Willcocks wrote: 'Bevan was less of an innovator than often credited. He created the National Health Service, but his debts to what went before were enormous.'
a List all the ways in which Bevan was important to the introduction of the NHS.
b List any ways in which he was a hindrance.
c Consider all the other factors that were important in the development of the NHS. How important was Bevan's contribution in comparison?
d Write an essay:
How important was Aneurin Bevan in the creation of the National Health Service?

5 What political methods did Bevan and his supporters use to try to defeat the doctors' opposition to the NHS?

6 Were the doctors really money-grabbers, trying to rob the poor of the right to health?

7 Working in small groups, compare the opposition of the 'dirty party' to Chadwick and the Public Health Board of 1848 (see pages 38–39) to that of the doctors to Bevan and the National Health Service in 1946. Can you find any parallels and similarities?
Write an essay:
Was 1946 a 're-run in different clothes' of the events of 1848?
Writing the assignment:
Devote a paragraph to each parallel or similarity you have found. For each, mention the events in both 1848 and 1946, drawing out and explaining the similarities. Then come to a conclusion about whether 1946 was *really* a 're-run' of earlier events, taking account of the different historical situations.

D A T A P O I N T

The welfare state

1944 *Education Act (England and Wales)*
Provides free secondary education for all children up to the age of 15.

1945 *Family Allowances Act*
More than 2.3 million families are given an allowance of five shillings (25p) for each child after the first.

1946 *National Insurance Act*
A weekly stamp (partly deducted from wages, partly paid by the employer) gives insurance cover for unemployment pay, sickness benefit and old age pensions.

1946 *National Insurance (Industrial Injuries) Act*
Persons permanently injured at work receive a pension.

1946 *National Health Service Act (England and Wales)*
Sets up a state medical service, including dentists and opticians, which is free and for all.

A central government Health Services Council is set up to co-ordinate the administration of the National Health Service (NHS), which is divided into three parts:
- 14 Regional Hospital Boards are set up in England and Wales to co-ordinate and improve all hospitals;
- 138 Executive Councils are set up to take responsibility for the GPs;

- each county has to create a Health Committee to administer the new health centres and services such as midwives, home nurses and health visitors, refuse collection, sewerage and food inspection.

1946 *New Towns Act*
'New towns' – for example, Stevenage, Basildon, Harlow, Newton Aycliffe and Peterlee – are planned to provide alternative housing to inner-city slums and decaying industrial and coal-mining villages.

1947 *Town and Country Planning Act*
The government sets a target of 300,000 new houses a year.

1948 *National Assistance Act*
Abolishes the Poor Law. Payments are made to those who need help but have not paid for it through National Insurance – for instance, the blind, deaf, crippled and mentally ill.

1948 *Children Act*
Local authorities are given responsibility to house, maintain and care for all children 'deprived of a normal home life', providing children's homes, nurseries, remand homes and foster-homes.

SOURCE 4

Newton Aycliffe in the 1980s
Council workers maintain a pleasant and healthy environment. Almost all the houses are council houses. Social amenities have been provided by the planners: on the left is St Clare's Church, behind it the primary school, and to the right the working men's club.

A cartoon view

Cartoons are a difficult and sophisticated type of political comment. They have to be interpreted; often the details are important. They are biased and present an extreme, caricatured version of one side of the argument only; for this reason they must be treated carefully by historians.

SOURCES A AND B

Both these Zec cartoons appeared in the *Daily Mirror*.

PUNCH OR THE LONDON CHARIVARI—APRIL 3 1946

MORITURI TE SALUTANT.

Punch, January 21 1948

DOTHEBOYS HALL

"It still tastes awful."

SOURCE C

A *Punch* cartoon of 3 April 1946. *AN:BEV:IMP* is a mock-Latin abbreviation standing for 'Aneurin Bevan Emperor'. The Latin phrase *Morituri Te Salutant* (Those about to die salute you) was what Roman gladiators said to the emperor before they fought to the death. The three gladiators' clubs are inscribed 'BMA'; their opponents' nets read 'State Control'.

Questions

1 Using pages 53–54, list the doctors' objections to the National Health Service Bill.

2 Divide into groups. Each group takes one cartoon. Write down a description of it in such a way that someone who has not seen the cartoon will be able to imagine what it looks like.

3 Then, working together, answer the following questions:
   a How does your cartoon represent the doctors?
   b How does it represent Bevan?
   c Is the cartoon on the side of Bevan or the doctors?
   d Explain the message of the cartoon, including the relevant details of the drawing.

4 In turn, share your findings with the rest of the class. For each cartoon, debate the question: 'How true is the cartoon to the reality?'

5 Then discuss as a class: 'Cartoons make no attempt to be fair. Are they therefore useless to the historian?'

6 Take one cartoon. Give written answers to Questions 1–5. Writing the assignment:
   Be careful to explain every point you make, referring to the picture.
   Question 5 is the most important. Remember in your answer to try to address the following issues:
   • what information the picture contains;
   • the bias of the cartoon, and how the historian copes with it;
   • what historians can use the cartoon to tell them;
   • how firm are the conclusions historians can make from the cartoon?

SOURCE D

A *Punch* cartoon of 21 January 1948. Dotheboys (pronounced 'Do the Boys') Hall was a school in Charles Dickens' novel *Nicholas Nickleby* in which a fierce, tyrannical master maltreats and bullies the pupils 'for their own good'.

E.H. Shepard, the artist who drew the *Punch* cartoons, also illustrated the *Winnie-the-Pooh* books for children.

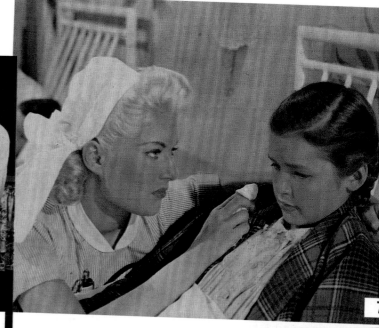

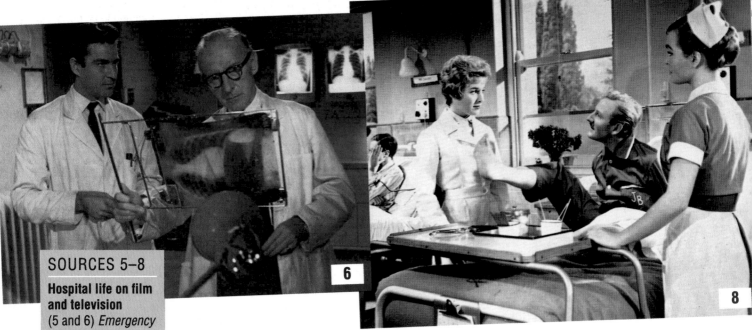

SOURCES 5–8

Hospital life on film and television
(5 and 6) *Emergency Ward 10;* (7) *The Feminine Touch;* (8) *Carry on Nurse*. Are pictures such as these entirely useless as historical sources?

A source of national pride

The National Health Service was immediately popular. On the 'appointed day' (5 July 1948) patients flocked to see the doctors, dentists and opticians. In the first year of the scheme 5,250,000 pairs of spectacles were issued and 187 million prescriptions for drugs were written out.

The NHS seemed to raise people's awareness of health issues. Before the war, health issues were dealt with by specialist medical journals such as the *Lancet* and the *British Medical Journal*, read only by doctors; after the war, thousands of housewives bought the BMA's promotional magazine, *Family Doctor*. Health became a media issue. In 1958 *Woman's Own* printed a series of 'moving dramas' about life in a general hospital. In the same year, BBC television showed a ten-part documentary series about the medical services called *Your Life in their Hands*. Television soap operas such as *Emergency Ward 10* attracted large audiences. There was even a 'Carry On' film, *Carry on Nurse*.

These developments were coupled with rapid advances in medicine, which seemed to make miracles possible (see **Datapoint: Medical advance**, right). There is no doubt that the public were proud of the NHS and thought it the best health system in the world (**Source 9**), although it is possible that the NHS was not as remarkable as they thought (**Source 10**).

SOURCE 9

For its customers [the National Health Service] was a godsend, perhaps the most beneficial reform ever enacted in Britain, given that it relieved so many not merely of pain but also of the awful plight of having to watch the suffering or death of a spouse or child for lack of enough money to do anything about it. A country in which such a service exists is utterly different from a country without it ... The people, not just some people, were being cared for.

P. Calvocoressi, The *British Experience 1945–75*, 1978. Calvocoressi is a British journalist and businessman.

SOURCE 10

The National Health Service ... reorganised but did not radically transform medical care in Britain. By the end of the war, the majority of workers were covered by National Health Insurance. Private insurance plans paid for doctors' services to most other people ... [However,] the NHS quickly became a symbol of the fairer social policy for which, many Britons believed, the war had been fought. Moreover, the NHS became a source of pride in a country exhausted by war, its empire and thus its trade dissolving, its industrial plant and labor force increasingly obsolete.

D.M. Fox, *Health Policies, Health Politics*, 1986. Daniel Fox is an American hospital administrator.

D A T A P O I N T

Medical advance

Life expectation at birth

	Male	Female
Iron Age Britain	29.5	26.5
Britain in 1961	67.9	73.8
Britain in 1991	73.2	78.1

Medical highlights of recent years

'With each new scientific development, medical practices of just a few years earlier become obsolete.'
Encyclopaedia Britannica, 1990.

1940 H.W. Florey (an Australian pathologist) and E.B. Chain (a German biochemist) discover how to mass-produce pencillin. Penicillin is extensively used during the Second World War to treat wounded soldiers who develop blood-poisoning.

1940s The New Zealand-born surgeon Archibald McIndoe does the first plastic surgery, on the faces of British pilots disfigured in the Second World War.

1948 In Britain, the surgeon R.C. Brock completes the first successful open-heart surgery to clear a blocked valve.

1950 In the United States, the first successful kidney transplant is performed.

1952 In Denmark, hormone injections are used to change the sex of Christine (formerly George) Jorgenson, an American soldier.

1955 The American doctor Joseph Salk produces a polio vaccine.

1955 The *Clean Air Act* imposes smokeless zones, reducing smog in Britain and, with it, the incidence of diseases such as bronchitis.

1957 A Medical Research Council Report claims that smoking causes cancer.

1958 Swedish doctors develop an internal pacemaker for the heart.

1961 The British molecular biologist F. Crick discovers the structure of DNA (the 'genetic code' of life).

1961 An oral contraceptive pill becomes available on the NHS.

1967 In South Africa, the surgeon Christiaan Barnard does the first heart transplant.

1969 A British woman has quintuplets after receiving fertility drug treatment.

1978 In Britain, Louise Brown – the world's first 'test tube baby' – is born.

1979 The British scientist G. Hounsfield invents the CAT body scanner.

1980 The United Nations World Health Organisation declares the smallpox bacteria officially extinct.

1980 In the United States, genetic engineers create interferon, a synthetic substance which kills viruses.

1981 Los Angeles doctors identify a new disease, AIDS.

1986 In Britain, Davina Thompson becomes the world's first heart, lungs and liver transplant patient.

Why did health improve?

We are much healthier than we were two hundred years ago. But what has caused the improvement in the nation's health? This issue is important for the question: 'What is to be done about the National Health Service?' (see pages 61–62: Criticisms and problems).

(see pages 61–62: Criticisms and problems)

SOURCE A

Medical progress?

It is only possible to recount here a few of the triumphs of modern medical research ... Probably sufficient has been said to indicate the nature and degree of decrease in disease and the improvement in health and physique made possible by the application of medical science in recent years.

Sir Edward Mellanby, *Recent Advances in Medical Science*, 1939. Mellanby was Secretary of the Medical Research Council. He advocated the importance of better food, milk and cod-liver oil for the health of children.

SOURCE B

Better health between the wars

There were many reasons for this improvement in the nation's health. The most important was probably the fall in food prices ... At the same time, wages continued to rise ... Better quality food was eaten by most people. This included more meat, fish, eggs and milk ... Whilst eating habits improved, drunkenness declined.

J. Salt and B.J. Elliott, *British Society 1870–1970*, 1975. Salt and Elliott are historians.

SOURCE C

Fashion?

The principal reason for the improvement was a change in fashion rather than a campaign for the public health. If the fashion of the day dictates that a young woman shall wear short skirts and short hair; that she shall appear in the open air and on the seashore in light and attractive clothing, then she must be clean. There is no alternative. Then the young men who parade on the beach will learn that they are unacceptable unless they also are (in the soap-and-water sense) fresh and clean.

J.M. Mackintosh, *Trends of Opinion about the Public Health 1901–51*, 1953. Mackintosh was Professor of Public Health at the University of London.

SOURCE D

The McKeown hypothesis

Except in the case of vaccination against smallpox ... immunisation and therapy [medical treatment] contributed little to the reduction of deaths from infectious diseases before 1935, and they were much less important than other influences.

T. McKeown, *The Modern Rise of Population*, 1976.

In order of importance the major contributions to improvements in health in England and Wales were from limitation of family size (a behavioural change), increase in food supplies and a healthier physical environment (environmental influences) and specific preventative and therapeutic measures.

T. McKeown, *The Role of Medicine*, 1976. McKeown was Professor of Social Medicine at the University of Birmingham.

Questions

1 Using Sources A–D, list all the causes that contributed to the improvement in people's health. Add ideas of your own if you wish.

2 For each cause, trace the linkages that explain how it led to better health. Remember the key-word 'so' (e.g. better food made people stronger, so their bodies were more able to fight off disease, and so they were healthier).

3 Look at the 'Medical highlights of recent years' in the **Datapoint: Medical advance** on page 59. For each, explain how it benefited humanity. In groups, brainstorm all the modern medical achievements you can think of. Analyse them, putting each achievement into different 'areas of medical advance'. Add the category 'Medical advances' to your list of the causes of the improvement in people's health.

4 McKeown claimed that immunisation and medical care were less important than other factors. Explain how the graphs (Source E) support his argument.

5 Discuss which factors in your list of the causes of improved health were the most important.

6 Show how certain of the causes on your list are connected.

7 Imagine that the government wishes to produce a publicity leaflet on its future plans for the NHS. The first page of the booklet is to be entitled: *Why Are We Healthier?* As the historian on the team, you have been asked to write this page. Your article must take account of all the different causes and how they improved health. It must use some facts and figures to prove the points, and make it clear which is the most important cause. You have space for 350 words and two small pictures. Submit a draft text to your editor. Attach your suggested pictures (with captions).

Criticisms and problems

From the start, the National Health Service faced problems, many of which, 50 years later, it has still not solved.

1 Structure

There was little co-ordination between the three administrative services – hospitals, GPs and local authorities – set up in 1945. In 1974, therefore, the Labour government re-organised the Health Service. Far from solving the problem, it merely turned the NHS into an unwieldy bureaucracy. The NHS was accused of inefficiency and waste.

2 Costs

In 1945 Beveridge had argued (as Chadwick had done in 1842) that the cost of the NHS would be paid back in the form of a healthier population, creating greater wealth. This proved to be untrue. National insurance contributions have never met the growing cost of the NHS, which has had to be paid for out of taxation. Unemployment and early retirement have meant that the increasingly heavy tax burden is being placed on a shrinking workforce. In addition, an ageing population creates its own medical problems; one-third of all medical expenditure on a person occurs in the last year of life.

3 Hospitals

In 1946 the opponents of the NHS had realised that it was not really a *health* service at all. It was a sickness service for people who had fallen ill; the NHS was primarily a hospital service. However, despite the vast amounts spent (see **Datapoint: The National Health Service** on page 62) many hospitals, especially the former Poor Law hospitals, continued to be housed in old buildings, and to be badly equipped.

Meanwhile, all hospital personnel felt aggrieved. Hospital doctors, paid far less than their colleagues in America, joined the 'brain drain' to the United States.

Nurses were badly paid, and hospital cleaners, porters and receptionists were amongst the lowest paid workers in the country; this led to a number of very damaging strikes in the 1970s and 1980s.

4 Illness

New (and ever more expensive) technology achieves medical miracles, but it creates as many problems as it solves. Premature babies who would have been brain damaged are now safely delivered; but premature babies who would have died now end up with brain damage. People in Britain rarely become ill and die from diptheria and TB, but they still become ill and die – from illnesses such as cancer, heart disease and, increasingly, AIDS, even though these diseases are connected to lifestyle and are avoidable. In the period 1976–91, the consumption of wine more than doubled (resulting in more car accidents, drink-related injuries and associated diseases such as cirrhosis of the liver) and the number of drug offences increased four-fold.

5 Inequality

The plan to redistribute doctors to the poorer areas of the country (see page 54) never materialised; a study in 1968 found that the 'underdoctored areas' were as underdoctored as ever. Of 169 doctors appointed to these areas in 1968–69, 164 came from abroad.

In 1977 the Labour government set up a *Working Group on Inequalities in Health* under the chairmanship of Sir Douglas Black. Its report (the *Black Report*) was published in 1980. It found that health (or lack of it) depends to a large extent on which social class you come from, and where you live. Families from social classes IV and V (unskilled or semi-skilled manual workers) suffered more low-weight births, more deaths in infancy, more accidental deaths, more deaths from cancer, heart and respiratory diseases, and more long-term illnesses and disabilities than other social classes. They were less likely to use services such as dentistry, immunisation and screening for cancer. They smoked more and ate unhealthily. The report found that in some respects their health had deteriorated since 1960. The mortality rate in the south-east of England was 26 per cent better than in the north. The report concluded that the cause of this was 'the class structure: poverty, working conditions, and deprivation in its various forms'.

6 Disillusion

By the 1980s many people had come to think that the National Health Service did not address the real causes of lack of health, did not direct care where it was needed, and had probably helped to create the carelessness about diet and lifestyle that kept people unhealthy.

Some critics went even further. In 1986 one historian argued that, after the war, Britain had wasted her resources on the welfare state, instead of investing in the modernisation of industry and technology. The welfare state, he said, had turned the working classes into:

> ... a subliterate, unskilled, unhealthy and institutionalised proletariat [working class] hanging on the nipple of state maternalism.

C. Barnett, *Audit of War*, 1986.

7 Which way forward?

In the 1980s some medical experts advocated a new approach to public health. Their argument ran like this:

- The NHS is really a sickness service, not a health service (see point 3).

- The NHS is failing to keep certain classes healthy (see point 5).

- It had been proved that a healthy, wealthy environment has the best effect on public health (see page 60).

They proposed, therefore, what they called 'the New Public Health' – to redirect the national health services towards health promotion: better welfare services, community health workers, better health education and health

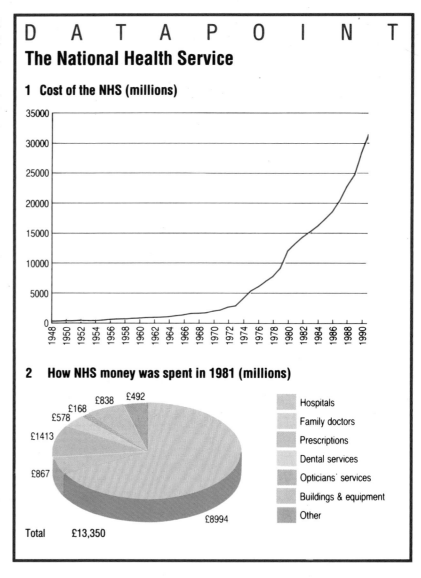

D A T A P O I N T

The National Health Service

1 Cost of the NHS (millions)

2 How NHS money was spent in 1981 (millions)

£492, £838, £168, £578, £1413, £867, £8994

- Hospitals
- Family doctors
- Prescriptions
- Dental services
- Opticians' services
- Buildings & equipment
- Other

Total   £13,350

centres (including swimming baths and gymnasia, as well as medical centres). The *Black Report* of 1980 wanted the government to provide free milk for all families with children, free school meals for all pupils, better health care services in schools, an enlarged programme of health education through the mass media, strict measures to stop smoking, and more spending on housing improvements. It was estimated that its recommendations would cost £2000 million a year.

Meanwhile, however, a new Conservative government had been elected in 1979 under the leadership of Margaret Thatcher. It advocated a different approach to the problem, privatising hospitals and urging people to take more care of their own health.

SOURCE 11

A modern surgical operation
Advocates of the New Public Health want to move away from expensive medical treatment to concentrate more on health promotion.

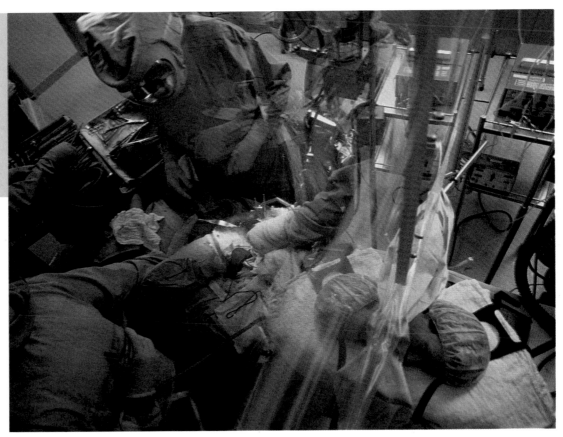

Knowledge and understanding

These questions will help you to investigate the long-term development of public health and medicine in Britain.

1 *What is to be done about the National Health Service?*
Discuss as a class:

a What are the most important problems facing the NHS? Find linkages between the seven problems outlined above (pages 61–62).

b Can we still be proud of the NHS? How far does it meet the criteria for a public health system that you developed on page 4?

c Is the 'New Public Health' the right way forward for the NHS?

d Some doctors have recently suggested that, since resources are limited, expensive treatment for the few should not be allowed to reduce standards for the many. They say we may have to learn to 'draw the line' – to turn off the ventilator for the baby that will never achieve full health, and refuse expensive operations for old people with only a few (unproductive) years of life left. Debate this point of view in class.

e Write to the Conservative, Labour and Liberal Democrat party headquarters, and ask for a copy of their manifesto for the National Health Service. Which, in the light of your study of medicine and public health, contains the most sensible proposals?

2 *Development through time*
Use the Index to track down all the references in the book to one of the following:
  life expectancy;
  doctors;
  hospitals;
  surgical operations;
  medical knowledge and treatments;
  hygiene and sanitation;
  attitudes to disease;
  housing.

Construct a date list of the most important developments. Use your date list to draw a timeline illustrating the development through time of the topic you have chosen.
Write an explanation of the timeline, under the title:
Progress in (your topic) through time.

3 *Causation*

a Use the Index to find all the ways in which war has influenced the development of public health through the ages.

b Write an essay:
How important was the part played by war in improving the health of the nation?

Index